DIGITAL PORTFLIOS

Powerful Tools for Promoting Professional Growth and Reflection

SECOND EDITION

Elizabeth Hartnell-Young
Maureen Morriss

Foreword by
Barbara Cambridge

CORWIN PRESS
A SAGE Publications Company
Thousand Oaks, CA 91320

Dreamweaver is a registered trademark of Macromedia, Inc.

ePortfolio Australia is a trademark of the ePortfolio Australia consortium in Australia.

Folio by ePortaro is a trademark of ePortaro, Inc.

Foliomaker is used with permission from Folios International Pty. Ltd.: www.foliosinternational.com

iPod is a trademark of Apple Computer, Inc., registered in the United States and other countries.

iWebfolio is a trademark of Nuventive.

Masterfile is a trademark of Concord USA, Inc.

Microsoft Word, Microsoft PowerPoint, Microsoft Internet Explorer, Microsoft FrontPage, and Windows are either registered trademarks or trademarks of Microsoft Corporation in the United States and other countries.

Netscape Composer is a trademark of Netscape Communications Corporation, which may be registered in other countries.

Palm and Pocket PC are among the trademarks or registered trademarks owned by or licensed to Palm, Inc.

The screenshot in Figure 5.4 is adapted with permission from Digital Principal Portfolio CD-ROM by David Stewart.

For information:

Corwin Press
A Sage Publications Company
2455 Teller Road
Thousand Oaks, California 91320
www.corwinpress.com

Sage Publications Ltd.
1 Oliver's Yard
55 City Road
London EC1Y 1SP
United Kingdom

Sage Publications India Pvt. Ltd.
B-42, Panchsheel Enclave
Post Box 4109
New Delhi 110 017 India

Printed in the United States of America

Library of Congress Cataloging-in-Publication Data

Hartnell-Young, Elizabeth.
Digital portfolios: Powerful tools for promoting professional growth and reflection/Elizabeth Hartnell-Young, Maureen Morriss.—2nd ed.
    p. cm.
Includes bibliographical references and index.
Rev. ed. of: Digital professional portfolios for change. 1999.
ISBN 1-4129-4929-7 or 978-1-4129-4929-3 (cloth)
ISBN 1-4129-4930-0 or 978-1-4129-4930-9 (pbk.)
1. Portfolios in education. 2. Digital media. 3. Educational technology. I. Morriss, Maureen.
II. Hartnell-Young, Elizabeth. Digital professional portfolios for change. III. Title.
LB1029.P67H37 2007
371.12—dc22   2006021820

This book is printed on acid-free paper.

06 07 08 09 10   10 9 8 7 6 5 4 3 2 1

Acquisitions Editor:	Cathy Hernandez
Editorial Assistant:	Charline Wu
Production Editor:	Beth A. Bernstein
Copy Editor:	Carol Anne Peschke
Typesetter:	C&M Digitals (P) Ltd.
Proofreader:	Dennis Webb
Indexer:	Karen McKenzie
Cover Designer:	Rose Storey

DIGITAL PORTFOLIOS

SECOND EDITION

Contents

Foreword

Connecting Ideas to Spur Thinking

A good book can stimulate a reader by providing new ideas, increasing understanding, making practical suggestions for action, challenging current presumptions, and reframing issues. This book will serve diverse purposes for its readers. Novices will be introduced to the wide scope of considerations regarding adoption of digital portfolios; experienced practitioners will find frames and matrices in which to identify their own practices in relation to those of others. A comfortable read that does not overuse jargon or dig too deeply into any one issue, this volume touches on many subjects that can spur further thinking and consideration in a reader's own context.

As a reader experienced with electronic portfolios, I found among many stimulating ideas in this book two particular spurs to thinking. First, Hartnell-Young and Morriss describe the feature of digital portfolios that distinguishes them from Web pages: Electronic portfolios have rhetorical purpose. They are designed on an occasion to move a particular audience for a particular purpose. The authors also take up the continuing debate about the possibility of an ePortfolio serving both formative and summative purposes. As I placed those topics side by side, I thought about the ways in which ePortfolios provide simultaneous practice in the process of making an argument about and for oneself and for the reader. This practice is good for the individual practitioner and for the reader.

The creation of an educational vision statement espoused by the authors challenges each portfolio maker to be explicit about desired outcomes of education. This statement forces the writer to identify the purposes and attendant goals of the educational enterprise in which the writer is engaged. At the same time, the vision statement differentiates the writer for the reader: What does this portfolio writer envision that will provide a context for all the evidence in the portfolio? Add to the educational vision statement the concept map that situates ideas and artifacts in relation to one another and to the vision statement, and the writer and reader both understand in a clearer way the direction and progress of the portfolio creator. This formative outcome is a learning experience for writer and reader.

Hartnell-Young and Morriss emphasize that self-managed evaluation is part of and aided by the ePortfolio process. A portfolio generator makes decisions about what he or she has learned, what artifacts demonstrate that learning, what needs attention in the future, and how current practice and evidence change past self-evaluation. Whether or not he or she uses rubrics to frame summative evaluation, the ePortfolio learner practices the feedback loop that characterizes effective assessment. When summative evaluation is necessary, for whatever reason, a reader can either see how effectively the person did self-assessment or view materials used for formative purposes within a structure built for summative ones. The writer may be responsible for repurposing the artifacts in a way that speaks to standards or expectations, but the writer is more able to take that step, having had practice in self-assessment for the purpose of learning about his or her own learning. Formative and summative assessment are both enhanced by the process of ePortfolio construction.

Second, this book posits that educators continue to grow professionally. Indeed, in the 21st century with its rapid change, they must, especially in the area of technology. Hartnell-Young and Morriss state, "A fundamental principle of this book is that educators grow professionally while producing digital portfolios." The authors claim that this growth comes from educators being producers as well as consumers of technology and from the deep learning associated with authentic work and critical commentary that are part of ePortfolios.

As I thought about this central need to grow professionally, I began to consider who helps educators grow. The authors remind readers that students often are more technologically savvy than their teachers. The terms *digital natives* and *digital immigrants* apply here: Students have grown up with technology, whereas many teachers are less acquainted with the culture of bloggers, gamers, and wiki participants. When Mary Catherine Bateson studied what high school seniors and college freshmen reported having taught their parents, technology was at the top of the list. Are teachers demonstrating their continual professional development to their students by soliciting student help with portfolio production? What better way to demonstrate life-long learning? In campus experience at the Carnegie Academy for the Scholarship of Teaching and Learning, students have played central roles in teaching teachers about what pedagogies work to help them learn. The same possibility exists for electronic portfolio construction.

Another source of professional growth for educators is peers. Hartnell-Young and Morriss emphasize the importance of communities of practice, pointing to the exciting practice of collaborative electronic portfolios as evidence of collective competencies of teachers in a networked model. The portfolio becomes a store of knowledge of a group, being both a corporate memory and an impetus for further progress. The authors cite McNair and Marshall's contention about portfolios in early teacher education: A portfolio can be "a digital profile of teaching experiences and reflections through which a community of practitioners can engage in online professional dialogue and support" (2006, p. 474). Colleagues in one of the Carnegie Academy clusters have developed the scholarship of teaching and learning as a networked practice. A natural auxiliary is a collaborative portfolio as a central feature for professional growth in a technologically permeated educational environment and society.

As electronic portfolio practice and research proliferate around the globe, it is important to record what practitioners and researchers are learning. Hartnell-Young and Morriss state, "At present, we rely on the reports of people involved in portfolio development to identify the learning that takes place rather than measuring the effect of portfolios directly. In the future, this learning might be measured in other ways." Fortunately, within the three cohorts of U.S., UK, and Canadian colleges and universities in the Coalition for Electronic Portfolio Research, institutions are documenting impacts of ePortfolios in systematic ways. However, that research and research being done in other sectors of education and parts of the world benefit from being based on effective practice, and *Digital Portfolios* will contribute to the knowledge base of practitioners beginning and further developing the effectiveness of their ePortfolios. I foresee that readers will make their own discoveries and their own connections as they explore this book. I'm sure that the authors will want to hear from those readers as we all continue our lifelong learning.

—Barbara Cambridge
Senior Program Officer, National
Council of Teachers of English,
Codirector, International Coalition
for Electronic Portfolio Research

Preface to the Second Edition

This book is designed for administrators, teachers, educators, graduates, and students with a passion for learning as well as for teaching. Those working in support roles, such as teacher assistants and administrative staff, can also benefit. This book provides readers with an overview of the framework and tools needed to develop a digital portfolio that records lifelong learning and professional growth and celebrates achievements.

In recent years, many institutions and software companies have recognized the opportunities for developing large-scale systems for digital and electronic portfolios (ePortfolios). In contrast, this book focuses on the person at the center of the process. Even those with little computer experience and limited equipment can use multimedia technology to create a vibrant, individualized, high-quality portfolio that can be continually and easily updated. Throughout the process, portfolio developers will gain greater knowledge of themselves and their learning processes while expanding technology skills. In addition, portfolio development can assist anyone preparing for performance review, looking for a job, or seeking a promotion. It also can help organizations aid their staff in focusing on development goals.

This book shows how to construct a portfolio, but it takes the portfolio approach further than the typical presentation folder. In our view, digital portfolios are linked with one of the urgencies of the 21st century: the need for administrators, superintendents, teachers, and students to better understand and use the possibilities of learning technologies. As explained in this book, the portfolio development process can help developers feel more confident with their technological skills, thus making them more open to sharing their skills and knowledge with others.

In many countries, portfolio development has become an important means of increasing organizational learning and effectiveness. This book raises issues that must be considered if a portfolio approach is to be pursued. People responsible for professional development and policy in education, whether in schools, school districts, or universities, will find the contents of this book valuable as they plan for professional and organizational growth.

This second edition reflects the explosion of work that has gone on in the field of digital and ePortfolios since the late 1990s. This is particularly evident in the range of software now available, making it easier to create professional products, even for those with very little knowledge of technology. Although the structure of the book reflects that of the first edition, many new examples have been included, and most chapters have been substantially rewritten to reflect recent developments. However, the fundamental values expressed in the first edition have not changed, and our recent work in the field convinces us that it is learning and professional growth that should be the focus of portfolio development in the 21st century.

Acknowledgments

Much of our growth and the ideas presented in this book would not have been possible without constant feedback and support from people all around the world. In our quest for professional growth we have taken some risks that have demonstrated to us the potential of collaborative professional development to create personal and organizational change. We always work to enable others to reach their dreams and aspirations, just as others have encouraged us with this project.

Since the first edition of this book was published, we have continued our journeys in new territories, and the portfolio movement has spread in various forms across the world. Many people involved in these developments have helped in the revision process by sharing their knowledge and perspectives with us. We are grateful to be part of this international community and thank all those who contribute to it and to our growth and development.

The original women@thecuttingedge, who began this journey with us, continue to be a source of inspiration. We particularly thank Janette Ellis and Charmaine Taylor for their contributions to the second edition.

Corwin Press gratefully acknowledges the contributions of the following reviewers:

Joanne Carney
Assistant Professor of Instructional Technology and
  Elementary Education
Western Washington University
Bellingham, WA

Faith Clover
Lecturer in Curriculum and Instruction
University of Minnesota–Twin Cities
Minneapolis, MN

Ralph Gilchrest III
Principal
Lake Gibson High School
Lakeland, FL

Debra Greenstone
Science Teacher
Mount Pleasant High School
Wilmington, DE

Sharon Jefferies
Third Grade Teacher
Lakeville Elementary School
Apopka, FL

Alexis Ludewig
Third Grade Teacher
St. Germain Elementary School
St. Germain, WI

Erin Powers
English Teacher
Paul Revere Charter Middle School
Los Angeles, CA

About the Authors

In the 1990s, Elizabeth Hartnell-Young and Maureen Morriss established a small team of teachers in elementary, secondary, and tertiary educational settings—named women@thecuttingedge—to develop a sample digital portfolio and stored it on CD-ROM. That innovation grew into a larger-scale professional development program, and they became convinced that given a realistic purpose, teachers do become highly motivated to learn more about technology and can achieve great things, which can, in turn, encourage student learning.

 **Elizabeth Hartnell-Young** is a research fellow in the Learning Sciences Research Institute at the University of Nottingham, UK. Her interests include teacher roles and professional development, ePortfolios, and mobile technologies for learning in schools. Her recent experience in developing and managing innovative projects in Australian schools includes the Boys' Education Lighthouse Schools Project in more than 350 schools.

Formerly a secondary school principal, she has also developed and presented numerous leadership and career development programs for the Australian Principals Centre, universities, and government departments. She is a founder of ePortfolio Australia™, a consortium of educators supporting professional development and research into portfolios, and has written numerous research reports and professional papers, including a chapter in the *Handbook of Research on ePortfolios* (edited by Jafari & Kaufman, 2006).

Elizabeth is also an honorary fellow in the Faculty of Education at the University of Melbourne, Australia.

SOURCE: Photo by Neal P. Kemp; used with permission.

Maureen Morriss is a 30-year teaching veteran, author, and influential educator throughout Australia who has held significant positions in the Australian Literacy Educators' Association and the Australian Literacy Federation. She began her career as an elementary school teacher in 1977 and quickly became a principal, curriculum consultant, and staff developer at the regional level. From 1988 to 2000, Maureen was a contract and tenured lecturer in Australian universities. In 2000, she joined A.U.S.S.I.E. Inc., a leading provider of customized professional development services for K–12 schools in the United States and abroad. She has worked extensively in New York City and in Montgomery County, Maryland, Hartford, Connecticut, and Fairfax County, Virginia, to provide instructional literacy leadership support to teachers, coaches, and administrators throughout these communities. She is the codeveloper and presenter of staff development programs and a four-year apprenticeship program across all District 20 schools. She created Balanced Literacy Informational Seminar Series (BLISS) for principals, now in its fifth year of use, and has acted as the regional leader for A.U.S.S.I.E. for New York City's Region 7.

Her passion is to make a difference in the lives of children through her work with other educators.

Introduction

Across the world, people are being asked to take responsibility for their own professional growth, understand more about themselves and their achievements, and take steps to develop new knowledge and skills. Teachers and administrators have found that producing a portfolio helps to clarify their values, enhances their capacity to reflect on their learning, increases their self-knowledge and self-esteem, and gives them added confidence in their work with colleagues and students. Authors such as Bridges (1997) believe that changes in the nature of employment mean that soon everyone will need a portfolio that demonstrates their skills, achievements, and particularly their versatility to achieve employment.

In his book *The Empty Raincoat,* Charles Handy (1994) says that intelligence has replaced land as the source of wealth. Knowledge workers—educated professionals and managers—own the new property. They can sell it, trade it, or give it away and, fortunately, still possess it. People in many countries can learn of the same new ideas at the same time and engage in meaningful conversations with others about these ideas around the globe.

In this context, teachers are in an awesome position. They have a great deal of knowledge and the skills to share this knowledge. Schools are centers of learning, and whole communities benefit from this learning. However, this can occur only if teachers understand their capabilities. Teachers in schools and universities, principals and superintendents, and support staff in educational institutions are being called on to demonstrate their knowledge. Each person brings a different combination of knowledge, skills, and experiences to their work. But it is not enough just to collect knowledge. Knowledge must be *used* in order to make a difference.

This book won't turn the reader into a designer. However, it will show educators how to use digital technology to describe their unique experiences and to reflect on how they grow and develop in their professional life. Portfolio development challenges developers to consider the impact of their work—how they make a difference.

Finally, this book will help teachers understand how technology might help them record and communicate their professional achievements and how they can share what they have learned with students to help them unlock the secrets of multimedia technology.

CHAPTER 1

Professional Learning, Portfolios, and Today's Technology

Many view the e-portfolio as the future of learning, a powerful aid for personal development.

৵ Tosh (2003)

Professional learning for teachers has always been important, reflecting the pace of change in education and society. For many years, teachers have had opportunities for professional development in the form of conferences and courses. The focus often was on providing information about curriculum innovations and specific classroom methods and practices that met the immediate perceived needs of teachers. Recently, the focus has been on longer-term learning, such as individual growth in self-understanding, setting goals for professional development, planning learning activities and projects, and reflecting on outcomes. Day (1999) argues that for school reform to be effective, learning opportunities for teachers must model constructivism, taking into account the individual learning styles and career history of teachers and contextual factors such as school culture, support of colleagues and leaders, and the influence of governments. In the constructivist view, teachers are always potential learners, able to make meaning out of experience individually and collaboratively. Day's definition of professional development is helpful:

> It is the process by which, alone and with others, teachers review, renew and extend their commitment as change agents to the moral purposes of teaching; and by which they acquire and develop critically the knowledge, skills and emotional intelligence essential to good professional thinking, planning and practice with young children, young people and colleagues through each phase of their teaching lives. (Day, 1999, p. 4)

School-based professional development therefore has become very important as teachers and their employers realize the value of learning situated in their everyday work setting. This demands that teachers work together to consider their learning within a purposeful framework, asking why they are pursuing an activity and, having learned something new, seeking to apply it to their work to benefit the community. By examining and reflecting on their work, teachers can learn more about their strengths and skills and about areas in which they can grow and learn. Such self-knowledge is an important tool that can be used to plan for further development. This type of professional learning has the dual purposes of improving or reforming schools while enhancing teacher skills, knowledge, and professionalism.

TEACHING AND LEARNING IN THE 21ST CENTURY

In the 21st century, valuing individual capabilities and talents is becoming more important than ever. Ways of organizing work are changing, making permanent employment less common and creating a sense of opportunity for some and great insecurity for others. Individuals are becoming increasingly responsible for managing their own career paths. According to Bridges (1997), the organization is no longer a structure built out of jobs but a field of work that needs to be done. Teachers are being asked to be self-sufficient and entrepreneurial and to engage in ongoing learning to keep up with change. The expectations of teachers' roles are changing for those preparing to be teachers, the institutions that train them, and the schools and communities that employ them.

Technology is also contributing to the changing expectations of teaching and learning. It has created wonderful opportunities for learning, and many teachers are working with students who are more familiar with technology than they are. With the recent information explosion, a teacher in the 21st century cannot possibly have all the information students clamor for. Many who have been teaching for more than 20 years are faced with the challenge of being learners at a time in their career when they hoped to be experts in their work.

As new skills and knowledge are needed for curriculum development and assessment, new methods of teaching and learning can be created as teachers and students use technology (Mercer & Fisher, 1998). Learning can be more fluid, for example, because they can be in contact after school hours, using online or cellphone technologies. However, the problem of data overload is real, and teachers are forced to make difficult choices about the use of technology, which can be used to support inquiry, link learners in many settings, and record and assess progress. Which of these should be emphasized? Trying out new things, gathering evidence, reflecting on activities, and making sense of the successes and failures are essential to the teacher's role of incorporating new technology to support learning. Exploring this method and the learning that results is important as teachers seek to develop useful resources for the future.

Teachers are knowledge workers: educated professionals with knowledge and expertise, dealing with the creation and communication of information. However, there is a digital divide: Access to a range of media is still limited for many teachers and learners within the one school, one city, or one nation. There are other practical barriers to professional growth. Often teachers are so busy with everyday work that they have little time to reflect deeply about or articulate clearly what they know. To overcome these barriers, it is essential for teachers to collaborate and for teachers and students to work together on their learning. Some teachers value this opportunity, as in this case:

> That relationship between the teacher as the provider of the information, the student as the person who absorbs it or learns it, that's completely changed. Everyone is just a learner and engaging in some sort of exchange, which I find excellent. I think some of the most interesting things I have learned about using computers, given that I would describe myself as an early novice in the area, have been things that kids have shown me. (Hartnell-Young, 2003b, p. 171)

A new term has arisen to describe this never-ending experience: *lifelong learning.* Lifelong learners, suggests Hargreaves (2004), know what they know, what they have to learn, and what they can do for an employer. This self-knowledge comes from spending some time reflecting on one's beliefs, values, and achievements, situating oneself in society. Teachers who engage in reflective practice spend time considering what they value as teachers and how this influences their approach to teaching, learning, their career paths, and their aspirations. Reflective practice includes recording thoughts, goals, successes, and failures. This allows teachers to understand more about themselves as learners and to communicate this to others. Some teachers write regularly in journals, others document critical incidents and their responses, and others collect snippets of information that are important to them in some way, such as quotes, photographs, or letters from students. Some make time to reflect with others, as one student told us

> I think you have to really reflect on what you are doing and why you are doing it, to make it important, make it worthwhile for yourself and for the people that you are teaching. When you have made those connections and reflections for yourself, it becomes real. Someone discusses it with you, a colleague talks to you about it and

you have a real sense of moving in the same direction.
(Hartnell-Young, 2003b, p. 226)

It is important to spend some time focusing attention on oneself, for as Stephen Covey (1992, p. 58) expresses it, "Until we take how we see ourselves—and how we see others—into account, we will be unable to understand how others see and feel about themselves and their world." One way to do this is to create a portfolio.

PROFESSIONAL PORTFOLIOS

Over the past two decades, as teachers have become more involved in planning, recording, and reflecting on their own learning, paper-based portfolios have been used as a means of keeping and presenting information about professional growth (Burke, 1996b; Wolf, 1994). However, paper-based portfolios have never achieved widespread adoption at higher levels of education (eport.consortium.org, 2003) because of significant cost and logistical barriers, and some believe that this type of portfolio is limited in that it typically captures only the final product rather than the interactions that lead up to the output.

With digital technologies, portfolios have become digital or electronic and are commonly known as ePortfolios (Greenberg, 2004). They are generally made up of a selection of artifacts in the form of digital files containing audio, visual, and textual material. The format of these ePortfolios ranges from highly structured and compartmentalized selections of artifacts to flowing narrative forms.

A portfolio can include statements of vision and values that describe and explain beliefs about education, indicate why various activities are included, and reflect on the outcomes of the activities and what was learned from them. The evidence can include curriculum materials or reports, photographs of students at work or the outcomes they produce, feedback from colleagues or employers, and even video clips of presentations.

WHAT EXACTLY IS AN ePORTFOLIO?

At present, there is much discussion about the need for clear definitions among those involved in large-scale portfolio projects. Here are some current ideas that, taken together, cover most of the aspects we believe are important.

- A digital repository with a purpose (Cambridge, 2003)
- A collection of authentic and diverse evidence, drawn from a larger archive, that reflects what a person or organization has learned over time, on which the person or organization has reflected, designed for presentation to one or more audiences for a particular rhetorical purpose (Educause, 2004)
- Privately owned, with complete control by the owner over who has access to what and when (Europortfolio, 2006)
- A toolbox for the student and the knowledge worker (Home & Charlesworth, 2004)
- An information management system that uses electronic media and services (Haywood & Tosh, 2004)
- A Web-based method to save work and information about your educational career (www.eportfolio.org)
- Digital stories of deep learning (Barrett, 2004)
- An inventory of acquired knowledge, skills, and abilities (Chang Barker, 2003)

Love, McKean, and Gathercoal (2004) make a distinction between ePortfolios and Web folios, suggesting that the former are stored on transportable media (e.g., CD-ROM, thumb drives, or memory sticks) and not accessible from the Web, but in this book we use the term *ePortfolio* to mean the container of items as qualified here, in all digital forms of representation.

ePortfolios link the need for professional development with the need for greater skills and understanding of technology. These digital portfolios require thoughtful construction and not only provide teachers with a vehicle to shape their goals but also help them further their goals by experiencing the potential of technologies for learning.

If you open up an ePortfolio, it might look something like Figure 1.1. This is why some people think an ePortfolio is equivalent to a home page on the World Wide Web. But this is merely the entrance to the ePortfolio.

In a thoughtful ePortfolio, we expect to find a clearly reasoned case related to its particular purpose, accompanied by relevant evidence and reflection. Unlike Web pages that can be viewed by anyone, the ePortfolio is designed with a particular audience in mind and is addressed to that audience.

Figure 1.1 Sample ePortfolio Home Page

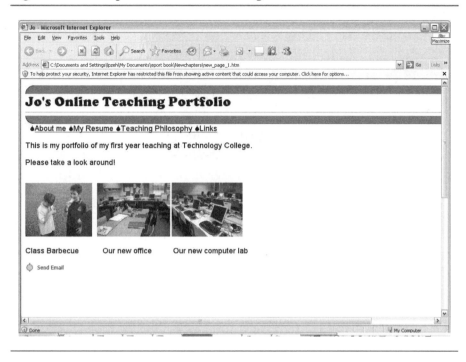

WHY CREATE ePORTFOLIOS?

Experienced teachers and administrators are finding that the benefits of developing a portfolio include the opportunity for professional renewal through mapping of new goals and planning for future growth. Many people discover that one of the most important and long-lasting outcomes of producing a portfolio is the self-esteem that comes from recording and reflecting on achievements and career successes and clarifying who they are as a professional and as a person.

Although there are many reasons to develop a portfolio, in this book we consider the developmental purposes as means for teachers to plan and reflect on their own growth. Many teachers and administrators are working in systems where personal accountability outside the classroom is becoming more controlled, and education administrators are using portfolios as containers of information for teacher assessment. For example, in New Zealand newly appointed principals are expected to complete a portfolio as evidence of their professional learning and progress related to their professional learning plan. Also, the portfolio is the basis for mentor and first-time principal discussions. First-time principals can also use their portfolio as valuable evidence of their annual performance agreement goals. The satisfactory completion of a portfolio is a requirement for a first-time principal who wants to receive the National Certificate of Principal Induction (University of Auckland School Leadership Centre, 2006).

Although these are legitimate uses for portfolios, when teachers perceive that accountability is viewed as more important than their knowledge and expertise, they can become cynical, and their portfolios tend to be heavy with documentation but light on passion. When teachers feel valued and rewarded, and then accountable, they feel more positive about their work. Therefore, this book focuses on the learning and development opportunities available to teachers, individually and in groups, through portfolio creation.

Digital stories and ePortfolios are forms for reflecting on and presenting the multiple identities of individuals and the collective identities of cultural, social, and work groups. As one teacher wrote

> Identifying skills such as teamwork, listening with empathy and understanding, interacting within the community, and being persistent, requires us to value and acknowledge diverse aspects of students' lives and interests. Students are encouraged to draw upon wider experiences that may well be found outside the school context, to create a richer picture of who they are. (Kane, 2004, p. 14)

It's not difficult to replace *students* with *teachers* in the preceding quotation to see the possibilities for portfolios in helping us all identify who we are.

From an individual's point of view, the multiple purposes for which portfolios are used are summarized in Table 1.1.

These purposes cover 10 areas:

1. *Professional development planning.* Many teachers undertake self-assessment activities as they set professional development goals and conduct research related to their teaching. The portfolio enables them to define their professional development needs.

2. *Recording of continuing professional development.* The portfolio can be used to record the steps in the process of professional development and reflections that teachers engage in along the way. The recording of all professional development activities, with an indication of time spent and learning outcomes achieved, often is suggested or required by school and professional associations.

Table 1.1   Purposes for Portfolios

Formative (Developmental) Purposes	Summative (Assessment) Purposes	Marketing Purposes
Professional development planning	University admission	Job application
Recording of continuing professional development	Course requirements	Cold calling
Celebration of achievements: lifelong learning	Performance review and promotion	Organizational capability
	Professional certification and registration	

3. *Celebration of achievements: lifelong learning.* Many people, including teachers, find that keeping a record of highlights of their formal and informal learning and achievements in a portfolio, with captions and reflections, is a wonderful boost to their self-esteem. In the spirit of lifelong learning, all residents of Minnesota (United States) and Wales are given the chance to create and administer their individual Web-based portfolios.

4. *University or college admission.* For many years, students in the visual arts have been expected to present portfolios of design, photography, or artwork in addition to their entrance interviews. Several projects in the United Kingdom are developing systems by which high school graduates can provide portfolios in addition to their examination scores to provide evidence of their capabilities.

5. *Course requirements.* Many university courses, particularly those for preservice teachers, require a portfolio that provides evidence of coursework and contains accompanying reflections. California Lutheran University uses a portfolio structure in the K–12 classroom context with some of its preservice teachers, inservice teachers, and graduate students.

6. *Performance review and promotion.* In many schools and universities, the presentation of a portfolio that provides evidence of meeting the criteria or standards often is required of staff in a regular review meeting. It is also

often required when an application is submitted for promotion. The Teaching ePortfolio at the National University of Singapore is designed to assess lecturers' teaching practices. Some people use portfolios to stimulate conversation and feedback between peers rather than from supervisors.

7. *Professional certification and registration (professional standards).* Some human resource, management, education, and health-related professional organizations have devised portfolio frameworks for their members in which they must provide evidence of achievement for membership, for continuing registration, or to upgrade their membership. Beginning and seasoned teachers in Australia and the United States often present portfolios showing how they have met the teaching standards.

8. *Job application.* Often applicants for a position prepare a portfolio providing evidence of skills, competence, and personal development. They take this to an interview, or even sometimes send it with the application. A good portfolio can make writing a résumé simpler.

9. *Cold calling.* Portfolios demonstrating skills and achievements have been used in the visual arts as part of the introduction process between client and artist. Entrepreneurial educators can use portfolios in a similar fashion to display their abilities when cold calling, or meeting a prospective client for the first time. When Kath graduated from her teacher education course in Australia, she sent a very professional ePortfolio constructed in Microsoft PowerPoint to prospective employers in Australia and overseas and quickly landed a job.

10. *Organizational capability.* Organizations can make important use of ePortfolios. They can use them to view the skills of their staff, evaluate programs, and market the capability of the school or organization to parents and the community.

The importance of purpose is expressed by David Baume:

Preparing a portfolio must always involve acts of judgment, periods of critical reflection, the processing of and learning from (mostly evidenced) experience. As a consequence, preparing a portfolio can be a moving experience—a long look into the mirror, with the image magnified and sharpened for greater clarity (sometimes welcome, sometimes not). But what form should the portfolio take? If the sole or primary intended function of the portfolio is, for example, for assessment, then the portfolio will take one form, usually the form of an evidenced claim that certain outcomes have been achieved, certain capabilities demonstrated. If the purpose is to plan for one's professional development, or to prepare and make a case for promotion, or to generate a growing journal of practice from which to learn, then a different form will be appropriate in each case. (Baume, personal communication, 2006)

Whatever the purpose, what is exciting and challenging is the ability to record, store, and present a portfolio in digital form. In order to do this, it is important to gather a wide range of evidence of work and accomplishments. Numerous commercial and open-source software tools enable this evidence to be stored systematically, but in the absence of these, anyone with a computer can organize digital files by categories in appropriately named folders. The skills needed to develop a digital portfolio are not complex, and the computer equipment in many schools and organizations is suitable, as can be seen in Chapter 2. You can see some excellent examples of digital portfolios from La Guardia Community College on the World Wide Web at http://www.eportfolio.lagcc.cuny.edu/.

Although people can develop ePortfolios individually, experience indicates that greater learning occurs when groups of people work together. The Internet is beneficial in this way because it allows communication between widely dispersed portfolio developers, allowing them to ask questions, share ideas, and provide feedback. This book advocates that anyone—teachers, students, and those outside formal learning situations—can benefit from preparing a portfolio in conjunction with other learners.

CHAPTER 2

Why Go Digital?

21st century literacy is the set of abilities and skills where aural, visual and digital literacy overlap.

        ❧ The New Media Consortium (2005, p. 8)

In this era of demand for computer-literate teachers, a digital portfolio provides powerful evidence that a teacher is not only confident with technology but becoming multiliterate. Students benefit from having teachers and administrators who are familiar with learning technologies and are able to use them appropriately in the curriculum. With these principles in mind, one way to introduce technology is to place the teacher at the center of the activity, to produce something that will be useful to the teacher and will increase her self-esteem. The digital professional portfolio, including a multimedia résumé, provides such an opportunity. Several types of software can be used to create portfolios. They can be broadly described as presentation (slide show), Web-based (using HTML), and database-driven software and are available commercially or as open-source products. Some are homegrown and used locally by schools and institutions, and others have wider reach across school systems and even nations. However, becoming computer literate is not the only reason for going digital. Many literacies can be enhanced through this process.

21ST CENTURY LITERACIES

Educators recognize that the concept of literacy has broadened with the spread of technologies. In response, the New London Group (1996) came up with the concept of *multiliteracies,* a term that acknowledges cultural and linguistic diversity and the communication opportunities we have through new media. Recently, the 21st Century Literacy Summit reported

> Unlike the traditional notions of language and literacy, which are primarily unimodal and textual, this new form of communication and self-expression occurs multimodally, incorporating visual and aural elements with textual elements, and an immediacy which itself is a dimension of the new language. Technology, which has done much to make the creation and dissemination of written communication a familiar everyday occurrence for most people, plays an especially important role in these new forms as well. Tools that allow sophisticated manipulation and creation of images, video, and sound are more and more commonplace, and they are especially

well known among those most fluent in these new language forms. (The New Media Consortium, 2005, p. 1)

People who are multiliterate can express themselves and make sense of the world through multiple modes: linguistic, visual, audio, gestural, and so on. Furthermore, they understand and control the media themselves so they can make informed decisions. Highly literate people can critique the content and effectiveness of the communication modes they have chosen to use and their appropriateness for particular audiences. One way to develop and practice these skills is by creating ePortfolios.

In a group of schools in Victoria, Australia, teachers worked together to create their own digital portfolios before requiring their students to do so. They reported that by designing and thinking through the concepts of their own portfolios, they engaged immediately with the concepts of multiliteracies and had to acquire skills they would be asking of their students, such as considering their intended audience, what they wanted to communicate, and how to do this most effectively. Many teachers chose to portray themselves as learners, with both peers and students as their audience. Initially they shared their portfolio presentations with one another for critique and feedback, later doing the same with their students (ePortfolio Australia, 2004).

The combination of text, graphics, sound, and video in digital form can be very powerful because it allows different perspectives on an aspect of a teacher's work to be displayed and reflected upon. The evidence can be presented to an audience in a multifaceted format, using text, photographs, sound, and video. This type of presentation capitalizes on Howard Gardner's (1984) work on multiple intelligences (Table 2.1) in that the material presented caters to multiple ways of sharing and understanding the vision, values, and achievements of teachers or administrators. For example, the textual aspect of a portfolio may appeal to a learner's verbal and linguistic intelligence because of the need to express growth and development via reflective comments. Another learner with a predisposition for visual and spatial learning may find that the digital images and nonlinear visual aspects of the graphics and video components suit his or her style. In this way, different aspects of the portfolio appeal to different learners. Table 2.1 demonstrates which aspects of multimedia can cater to specific intelligences.

Table 2.1   How Multimedia Can Cater to Gardner's Multiple
Intelligences Theory

Intelligence	Description	Multimedia Contribution
Logical and mathematical (scientific thinking)	This intelligence deals with inductive and deductive thinking and reasoning, numbers, and the recognition of abstract patterns.	Text and data Tables and graphs Comparative analysis of teacher's work over time Links to related documents
Verbal and linguistic	This intelligence is related to words and language, written and spoken.	Text, both written and oral Creative forms of expression Sound Variety of text forms, formats, fonts, and design
Visual and spatial	This intelligence relies on the sense of sight and the ability to visualize an object.	Graphics Links within the portfolio and to other sites Logos, images Creative forms of expression
Bodily and kinesthetic	This intelligence is related to physical movement and the knowings and wisdom of the body.	Producer is learning by doing Ability to move through the portfolio (not a static page) Video and animation
Musical and rhythmic	This intelligence is based on the recognition of tonal patterns, sounds, and a sensitivity to rhythm and beats.	Sound that captures mood, style, and feelings Video
Interpersonal	This intelligence operates primarily through person-to-person relationships and communication.	Photographs of self Photographs of others involved Comments about self and feedback from others
Intrapersonal	This intelligence relates to inner states of being, self-reflection, metacognition, and awareness of metaspiritual realities.	Reflection by self and others Planning and production entails metacognition Integration of values and action through linked material
Naturalist	This intelligence relates to recognizing relationships and systems in one's environment.	Organization of materials and links into a system of levels of information

EXAMPLES OF DIGITAL PORTFOLIOS

In the next pages, we show some sections of portfolios created in various digital formats and point out some of the benefits and opportunities for further development.

Some of the most powerful digital portfolios have been created as slide shows, as in the series of screenshots from a teacher's portfolio (Figure 2.1). Here Victoria, a preservice teacher, has created a structure that is always shown on the left side, with

Figure 2.1 Pages From a Preservice Teacher's Portfolio

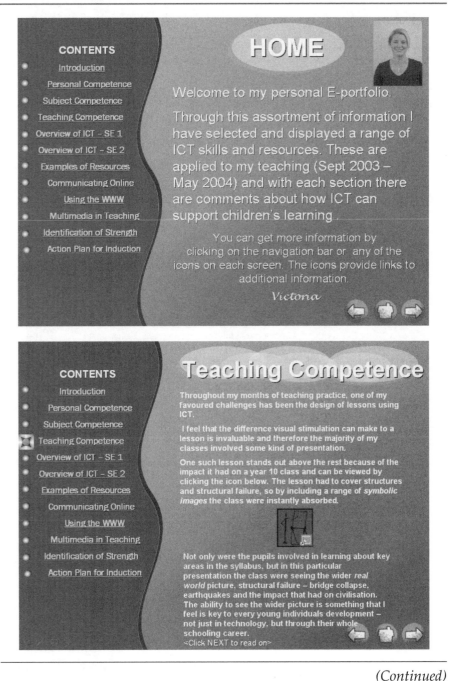

(Continued)

Figure 2.1 (Continued)

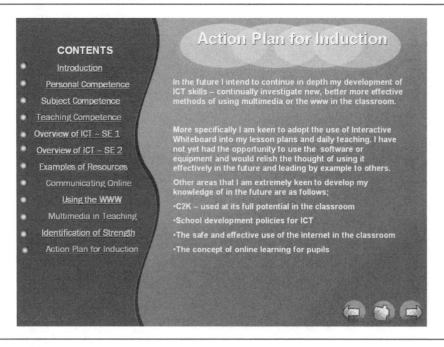

SOURCE: V. McAuley, PGLE Technology and Design, University of Ulster; used with permission.

Figure 2.2   Jo Educator's Portfolio Entry Page

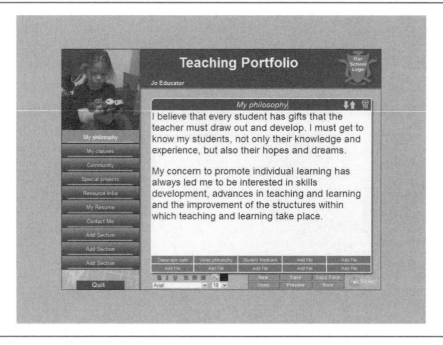

SOURCE: Used with permission of Folios International Pty Ltd. www.foliosinternational.com.

specific content and evidence on the right. The final slide shows her action plan for technology use in her first teaching post.

Figure 2.2 shows part of a digital portfolio that was created using a purpose-built product and saved to a CD-ROM. Each section on the left-hand side is set up as a clickable link to further information, which the teacher selected from an archive. The links at the bottom of the page open up artifacts that support Jo's philosophy.

Web-based (HTML) software often is used to create digital portfolios. These are designed simply to be viewed through Web-browsing software. In our early days of digital portfolio development, we used a commonly available Web authoring software program to develop simple yet functional HTML portfolios. They do not need to be on the World Wide Web to be viewed; they can be stored on a CD-ROM, DVD, memory stick, or other portable device.

In Figure 2.3, we show a page from a Web-based digital portfolio containing a photo of the teacher that is linked to a video file in which Janette introduces her philosophy of teaching. She also sets out her theme: managing change through leadership

Figure 2.3 An Experienced Teacher's Portfolio Entry Page

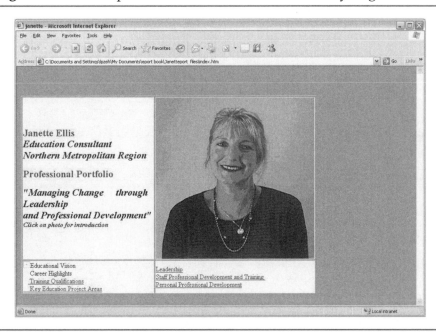

SOURCE: Used with permission of Janette Ellis.

and professional development. From this page, she has created hypertext links to her qualifications, project areas, and related examples of her work.

Hypertext is the language system often seen on the Internet as colored and underlined words that can be selected to reveal further layers of information. It enables the material in this portfolio to be linked to create a pathway through artifacts, from summary statements to complete documents, related items, and reflections.

Figure 2.4 shows two pages from Janette's portfolio containing artifacts and reflections on student-generated material, used in the portfolio with permission. In this section, Janette has deliberately developed the section "Assessing Students' Writing" for the purposes of expanding both teacher and parent perceptions and as a means to stimulate discussion around the nature of

Figure 2.4   Analyzing Student Samples in a Teacher's Portfolio

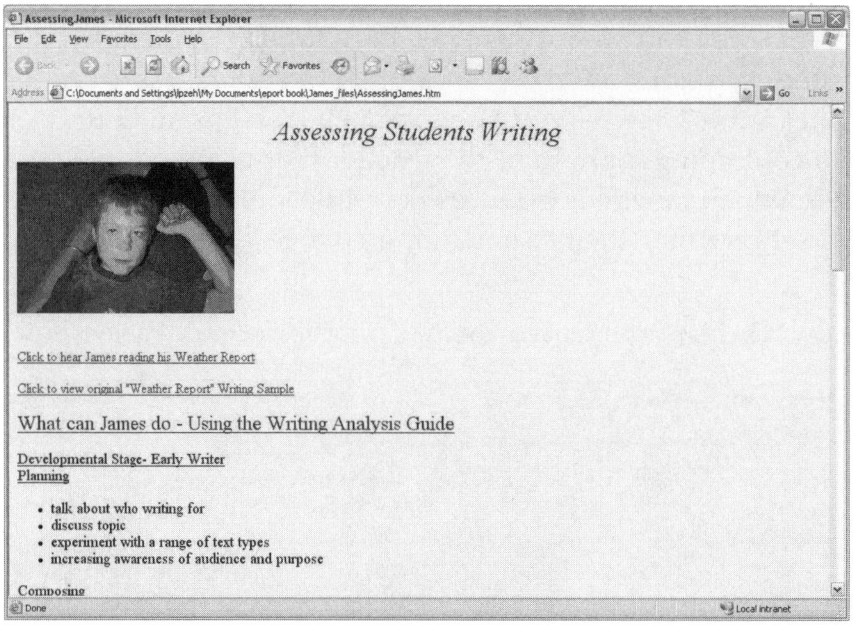

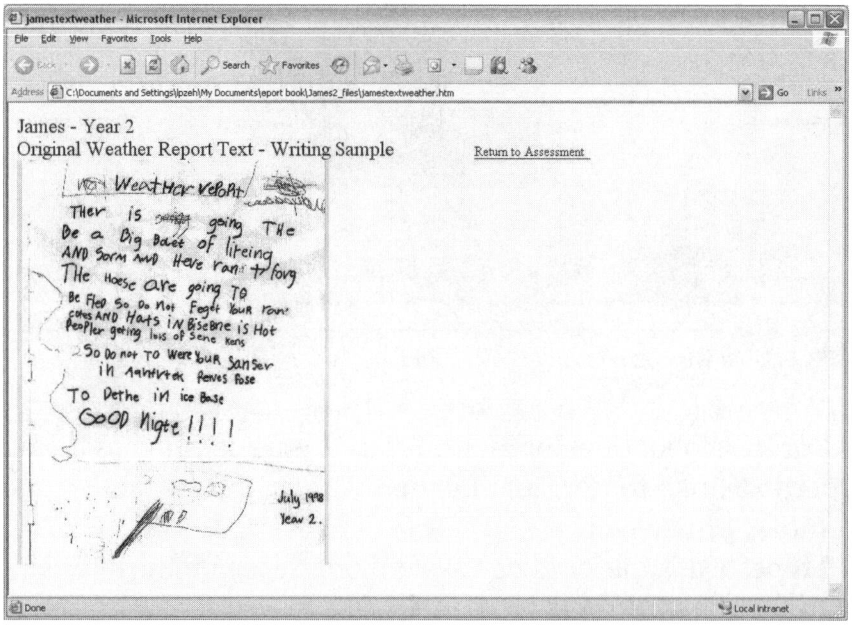

SOURCE: Used with permission of Janette Ellis.

student learning. This has proved to be a very powerful learning experience both for the teacher and for the audiences of peers who have viewed the sequence.

Seven-year-old James's task was to write and record a news-style weather report. The portfolio includes two artifacts he created: a sound recording of him reading his own piece of writing and the actual writing sample. They are indicated on the page by two links: "Click to hear James reading his Weather Report" and "Click to view original 'Weather Report' Writing Sample." The audio captures a confident, fluent reading, delivered with humor. The writing sample shows a range of skills and quite a few errors and often comes as a surprise to the audience. Through the link "Writing Analysis Guide," the teacher shows how to diagnose the problems and offers suggestions for moving James forward. The individual reflection is important for the teacher herself, and the whole sequence is valuable for shared learning for teachers.

Numerous ePortfolio software systems are built on databases that store the artifacts. A search of the Internet will reveal the products, both commercial and open-source. Open-source means that the software is free, and users contribute to improving it. The ePortfolios created in this way look similar to those in this chapter.

Viewing digital portfolio screens printed on the pages of this book is not the best way to understand how they display a range of literacies. Those interested in active ePortfolios and how the software works can refer to Helen Barrett's explorations in creating her own ePortfolios using many of the tools available today. These are found on the Web at http://electronic portfolios.org.

The idea of creating a digital portfolio might seem daunting for those who have little experience with technology. We have found that, given time and support, teachers are able to produce portfolios that include still images and video clips, reflective writing, and self-evaluation (Hartnell-Young & Morriss, 1999). Producing digital portfolios enables teachers to become more comfortable with computer equipment and its capacity, the uses of common software applications, and some of the potential of the Internet. This should lead them to use appropriate technology in the classroom for preparing materials, researching new information, and working with students in a range of formats.

It is appropriate and fun to involve students in the recording and collection of artifacts on some occasions and to share with them the reasons for the collection. For example, with their teachers' permission, students can videotape teachers engaged in classroom activities, devise projects that observe and reflect on their learning processes, and collect data to monitor classroom interactions. They can use mobile phones (cellphones) or PDAs with cameras and audio recording facilities to create rich repositories.

Feedback from students and colleagues should be considered and valued. Modeling recording and reflection to students demonstrates the importance of these activities, and this can encourage a dialogue with students about learning processes.

School administrators find that encouraging teachers to produce portfolios not only provides the benefits mentioned earlier but also can lead to a greater understanding of the skills and talents of the teachers and the intellectual capital in the organization. Some schools encourage teams to produce portfolios around particular projects, and others develop digital marketing packages to promote the school curriculum, personnel, and facilities.

The benefits of developing digital portfolios are summarized in Table 2.2.

Table 2.2   Benefits of Portfolio Development

Benefits for Educators	*Benefits for Organizations*
• Teachers can present a wide variety of evidence, linked for easy access.	• The process increases teachers' confidence in implementing technology.
• Teachers increase skills and knowledge of digital production.	• Students see a positive role model when teachers work with technology in this way.
• Evidence displays a range of literacies.	• Students and teachers work together on meaningful activities.
• Evidence addresses a range of audience intelligences.	• Students and teachers learn together when they create portfolios, enhancing the learning organization.
• Evidence can be shown to be authentic.	
• The portfolio enhances the image of the teacher as an innovator.	• The organization increases knowledge of its intellectual capital.
• The teacher becomes more employable.	• The product can be used to market the capabilities of the organization.

Developing a digital portfolio can be challenging, requiring teachers to model learning, develop technology skills along with their students, and share the results with a wider audience. Although they can be produced by teachers working alone, portfolio projects also are ideal for teams. Digital portfolio projects can benefit from the diversity of skills of team members as they act as coaches and mentors for each other. The outcomes include enhanced technology skills, understanding new ways of teaching and learning, and professional portfolios that effectively capture the knowledge and capabilities of the teachers who produce them. Chapter 3 explains how to get started on portfolio production.

Looking Forward, Looking Back

Integrating Personal Vision Into Your Portfolio

First we may ask, who are we, and what are our gifts? What are our distinctive competencies; what do we have to contribute that is unique or different? What special knowledge do we have? What do we value? What do we believe in?

⤷ Harrison (1984, p. 107)

Educators around the world realize that today's workplaces and communities need citizens who can increase their knowledge from many different perspectives, who can continue to learn in a rapidly changing environment, and who can think critically and strategically to solve problems. Citizens of the 21st century must be prepared to collaborate locally and around the globe, and the implications of this need to collaborate in teaching and learning are a constant topic of discussion. What should teaching and learning be like in the digital age? What do I value as a teacher? What knowledge is important? What is the role of technology in learning? How are schools preparing their students for a global future? These are some of the fundamental questions teachers and administrators are considering as they face the future. This chapter focuses on ways to articulate a vision, reflect on oneself, and track responses to these questions as a means of demonstrating professional growth. Records of this information and reflection can be stored in a personal archive. This archive, a professional history, will help educators better understand themselves and their roles to help them make positive contributions to the future.

FOCUSING ON VISION

For educators, the future is as important as the present. If not, why would they expend so much energy on understanding the needs of their students and preparing learning activities to extend their skills and knowledge? School administrators are expected to develop a shared vision with staff, students, and parents that guides and links the community. To achieve this, each person must be able to clarify and contribute a personal vision. As Fullan (1995, p. 13) states

> Shared vision is important in the long run, but for it to be effective you have to have something to share. It is not a good idea to borrow someone else's vision. Working on vision means examining and reexamining, and making explicit to ourselves why we came into teaching. Asking "What difference am I trying to make personally?" is a good place to start.

Writing an educational vision statement is at once a challenge and a valuable activity for all teachers. It forces them to clarify what they are working toward and to articulate goals that can be shared and debated with colleagues. An educational vision statement will change as goals are achieved and new targets are set. The vision is directed toward the future, but it must be undertaken in the present. In other words, the teacher must act on the vision from the moment it is conceived. As teachers engage in portfolio development, they consider the congruence of their vision and actions. From time to time, an updated vision statement can be saved in the personal archive.

Teachers who embark on portfolio development to plan and record professional growth are modeling a way of integrating vision, values, purpose, and action. Senge (1994, p. 141) uses the term *personal mastery* to describe the attitude of such teachers:

> "Personal mastery" is the phrase my colleagues and I use for the discipline of personal growth and learning. People with high levels of personal mastery are continually expanding their ability to create the results in life they truly seek. From their quest for continual learning comes the spirit of the learning organization.

Learning to develop a digital portfolio enables teachers to take risks with technology and to better understand its demands as well as its rewards. By capturing the experience of the learning journey, reflecting on its meaning over time, and sharing the learning with others, teachers develop new insights and understanding. Access to technology is enabling individuals and groups to implement change in both the philosophy and practice of teaching. However, technology should support rather than drive the curriculum, the learning environment, and professional development. A teacher's digital portfolio is not expected to be a graphic designer's dream; the emphasis should be on learning.

KNOWING ONESELF

Personal mastery begins with knowing and understanding oneself. For educators, knowledge of the values that underpin vision and knowledge of how we learn are two important aspects of self-knowledge.

Values are the ideals that give significance to our lives, which are reflected through the priorities we choose, on which we act consistently and repeatedly. A portfolio is one means of communicating these to others.

For those seeking professional growth, consideration of learning styles is another important aspect of self-knowledge. There are numerous tools, of varying quality, to assess learning styles, and many are available on the Web. Kolb (1984) identified four styles:

1. Diverging: combines preferences for *experiencing* and *reflecting*
2. Assimilating: combines preferences for *reflecting* and *thinking*
3. Converging: combines preferences for *thinking* and *doing*
4. Accommodating: combines preferences for *doing* and *experiencing*

The online Honey and Mumford questionnaire can help identify preferences in four domains based on Kolb's model: activist, reflector, theorist, and pragmatist (http://www.peterhoney .com). Recognizing learning style preferences can help teachers find appropriate professional development activities to meet their learning needs and build on their strengths. The areas of lower preference provide opportunities for further development.

Tools such as those referred to in this chapter help teachers better understand themselves and their multiple audiences. Because portfolios should be designed to communicate with people with different learning styles, it is important to step into the shoes of the audience by taking these differences into account.

GATHERING MATERIAL FOR A PERSONAL ARCHIVE

The personal archive is a personal evidence base that includes items such as those listed in Table 3.1.

Some simple methods of digitizing and storing graphic and sound material efficiently are described here.

- *Scanning text and images.* There is no need to retype printed documents. Papers or selections from documents can be digitized using a scanner. The scanning program will display instructions on your computer screen. Drawings, paintings, and newspaper articles also can be scanned or photographed. When scanning hand-written letters, cards, or photographs, follow the instructions, and the documents will be stored as digital image files. These

Table 3.1   Possible Items in a Personal Archive

Author	Self	Students	Parents, Teachers, Community
Personal characteristics and values	Vision statement dated Values exercise dated Self-assessments Goal statements Professional development plan Résumé Reflection	Letters Testimonials Cards Gifts	References Letters Awards Certificates
Classroom activities	Curriculum materials Lesson plans Case writing and notes of observations Photographs and videotape of activities and products Reflective writing	Examples of student work Tests Student self-evaluations and learning logs Evaluations and feedback of teacher Photographs of bulletin boards	Newspaper reports Television footage Thank-you letters
Schoolwide policy and programs	Policy documents Committee reports and records showing roles and responsibilities Press releases Reflective journal	Opinion surveys Articles in newsletters Photographs of extracurricular activities	Opinion surveys Statistics
Contribution to the profession and wider community	Articles in professional journals and books Presentations to colleagues and peers Memberships		Awards

can be inserted into other documents or into portfolios. Graphics are best saved as GIF or JPEG files if they are intended for use on the Internet because they take up less space than other formats. This can be done by selecting the GIF or JPEG option in the scanning program.

- *Digital stills and video.* Digital cameras are becoming more common as a means of photographing directly to memory stick rather than to film, thereby saving time. Images and video clips can be downloaded from the stick to the computer for use in documents. Images and digital video clips to be stored in the personal archive should be clearly identified with the date, event, names, and any other useful information to allow easy access during production. Some presentations or activities are best communicated through visual and verbal information, making video the perfect medium. Just as sports coaches have used video for many years to identify strengths and weaknesses and to record change over time, sometimes a few minutes of video are enough to assist a teacher in the quest for self-awareness and to suggest areas for development.
- *Audio.* Many forms of sound can be readily recorded on a portable digital recorder. In addition, many computers can record sound through a small microphone if they have the correct software and a sound card, which most computers now come supplied with. The computer microphone works similarly to a tape recorder, and the instructions for use are shown on the screen. Saving sound files is just like saving text or video files. Students might be taped giving class presentations, performing a musical composition, or singing in various languages. Teachers could also record themselves presenting papers at conferences or to a group as a way of reviewing and documenting their communication skills.

Because graphics, sound, and video files take up more space than text, they take longer to access than text files when viewed on the Web. It is wise to use highlights rather than the complete record when compiling a portfolio. Once teachers have gained experience in these areas, they will have options for production of portfolios, classroom materials, or presentations.

As the material is collected and stored, it is important that sufficient detail about the items, including both the scope and the impact of the activity, is recorded for future use. This can be easily done in many software systems through a process of tagging with metadata, which makes it possible for individual artifacts to be found easily. For more detail, contextual notes should be kept with each artifact. For example, is the date clear? How many students were involved? How many staff members? What role did the teacher play? What were the outcomes in the short or long term? Teachers are engaged in activities at many levels: classroom, teaching team, school, local community, state, national, and international. Table 3.1 also provides a framework to make sure that the artifacts reflect this range. This can be particularly important as teachers move toward leadership roles.

Many software systems allow digital files to be stored under categories established to suit the user's needs. In Figure 3.1, the categories for artifacts stored on this personal computer are Collaborative Leadership, Communication, Student Outcomes, Performance Targets, and, for the difficult-to-classify artifacts, a folder called Unclassified Bits and Pieces.

Without good organization, the amount of evidence in an archive can quickly become unwieldy. Some people arrange material chronologically, others by project, and others according to standards and competencies, as in Table 3.2. The system of organization is a personal decision, but it is important that information can be retrieved quickly.

BE PREPARED FOR THE "PORTFOLIO MOMENT"

Figure 3.1 Digital Folders Provide Clear Organizing Structures

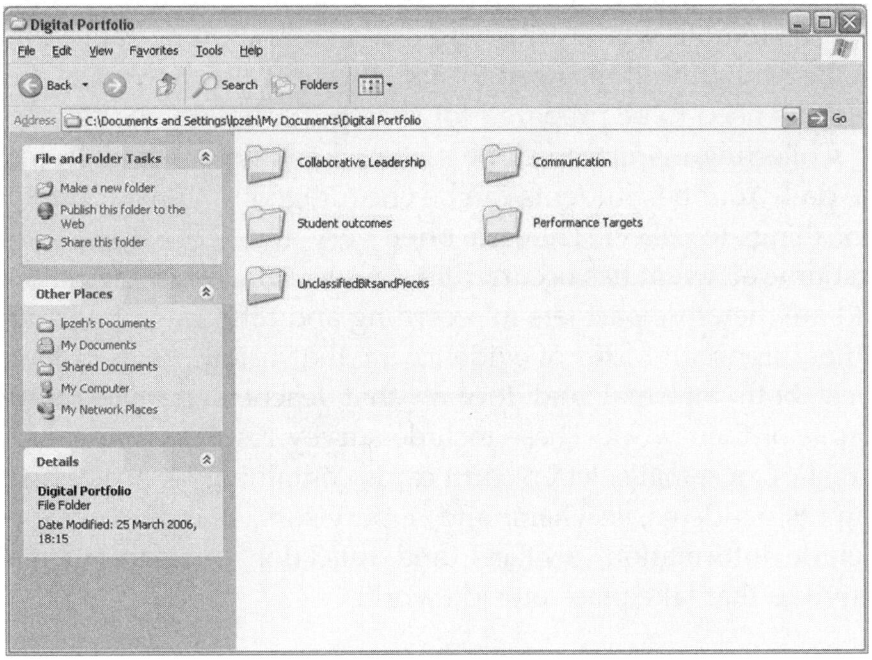

Table 3.2   Possible Structure for a Portfolio

A program designed to support school principals in New Zealand uses the following broad headings for the portfolio structure:

- Lead, coordinate, and facilitate the learning community
- Manage and develop the school culture
- Take responsibility for the school communication networks
- Play a figurehead role in representing the school
- Personal professional development
- Performance agreement objectives and goals

SOURCE: University of Auckland School Leadership Centre (2006).

The possibility of just-in-time digital capture of evidence requires a new mindset in relation to a teacher's daily work. Digital still and video images of classroom activity and products, presentations to other teachers, and even ideas for learning can be recorded easily if a small camera is available. These can be downloaded to a computer later, for storage in a personal archive. With a mobile camera phone they can be immediately sent to a Web server (to a site such as http://www.flickr.com/). The teacher in Figure 3.2 also used camera phones with his students to capture material for their portfolios. Similarly, teachers can make short notes of memorable occurrences on a handheld device such as a Palm Pocket PC, which can also be synchronized with personal archive folders on a local or remote server. Teachers can also audiotape reflections on the run without the need to stop and find a spot to write. But teachers need to be prepared for the "portfolio moment."

Collecting evidence can be a shared activity, integrated into the daily routine. Students can be encouraged to think of important things to collect. They are often very aware of "firsts"—the first time an event has occurred in their learning or in the class—and are therefore partners in recording and reflecting on history. Other important forms of evidence are the various items of feedback, both informal and formal, that teachers receive in the course of their work. These include survey results, comparative statistics, or e-mails, letters, and cards containing feedback from parents, students, teachers, and supervisors. It is also wise to include information, artifacts, and reflection on learning and activities that take place outside work.

Figure 3.2   Teacher Collecting Portfolio Evidence on His Camera Phone

SOURCE: Steve Lewis, Year 6 Teacher, Brighton Grammar School, Victoria, Australia; used with permission.

PERMISSION TO USE ARTIFACTS

It is essential to consider the rights of others when collecting artifacts. This is not only a courtesy but often a legal requirement. The use of photographs is essential in a digital portfolio, but they are a particularly sensitive area. It is wise to ask permission before taking a photograph of people, and any published photograph (including in print or on the Web) should include people only if permission has been granted. The laws relating to privacy, copyright, fair use, and intellectual property differ in various jurisdictions, so they must be checked, particularly before material is published. Permission to reproduce, quote, or refer to the work of others, including students, must always be gained before publication. A sample form is shown in Figure 3.3.

In some cases, teachers have not kept records or have moved from one school to another, leaving important evidence behind. If this is the case, reflective writing can help to keep the experience alive. Although there might not be a specific artifact

Figure 3.3   Permission From Teachers, Students, Parents, and Others to Use an Artifact in a Portfolio

[Address and Date]

Dear _____

I am compiling a digital portfolio for the purpose of _____ and seek your permission to use items as indicated.

☐ A photograph of you (attached)

☐ A video clip that includes images of you (attached)

☐ A piece of your writing

☐ A photograph or video of work you created

☐ An audio file of you speaking or singing

☐ Other _____

Your name will not be used unless you expressly wish it.

The portfolio will be available on _____ [e.g., CD-ROM, DVD, Web] and will be viewed by

☐ My colleagues and students at _____ [organization]

☐ My employer at _____ [organization]

☐ Unknown audiences on the Web at _____ [URL]

If you consent to this, please sign and date below.

Thank you for your contribution to my professional development as a teacher.

[Name] _____

I, _____, consent to the use of the items indicated above in the digital portfolio of _____. I consent/do not consent to my name being associated with these items.

_____ [Signature]

_____ [Date]

to represent an activity or event, reflections on what was intended, what was learned, and how this relates to the present are valuable and can be included in the archives. Fortunately, many schools also have archives. School archives may contain photo albums and press clippings of important school activities in recent years. If material from the recent past is not available, begin recording for a personal archive in the present.

REFLECTION

Lifelong learners are said to be reflective and self-directed, active investigators and problem solvers, and effective communicators, among other things. Digital portfolios have the potential to meet these needs, too; they should encourage reflection on life and learning, suggest opportunities for action, raise problems to solve, and offer flexibility of presentation to communicate to a range of audiences.

One teacher used his electronic daily schedule of classes, meetings, and communications as an artifact that recorded his contribution and a means of verifying that he was on task. When he reflected on this archive, he noted themes in his evidence, stating, "I've got patterns. And meetings, while I'm teaching. I think this week alone I've had 8 meetings so far, they're all there. If your boss said 'what are you doing?,' it's all there" (Hartnell-Young, unpublished research, 2005).

Schön (1983) describes two forms of reflection: reflection in action and reflection on action. Teachers often engage in the former as they act flexibly or think on their feet, but it is the latter—the systematic and deliberate thinking back over one's actions—that is encouraged during portfolio development. Baird (1991) advocates reflection as a means of progressing toward more purposeful teaching and meaningful learning. He asserts that reflection can be both introspective and outward looking, depending on the purpose and focus. A teacher might focus on specific personal performance or on his or her own learning abilities or might explore the meaning of an event, policy, or idea.

Writing reflections is seen to be important and does not take long periods of time; we have observed teachers engaging in valuable reflective writing over periods as short as 5 minutes. Lukinsky (1990) suggests that such reflective journals are a tool for connecting thought, feeling, and action. The popular freeform Web log (blog) containing reflection on the day's events or important themes is a form of reflective writing that might suit some teachers. Blogging can support learning in a flexible way (Maag, 2004) and therefore is a natural adjunct to portfolio development.

It is helpful to choose strategic evidence such as student work, videos, and teachers' notes and to analyze them in collaboration with other teachers. Focusing on the artifacts helps keep the professional conversation on track (Ball & Cohen, 1999). This method could well extend to teachers discussing evidence with their students.

The New Zealand program mentioned in Table 3.2 also provides a structure to guide action and reflection in a reflective journal. Collaborative leadership is one aspect, defined as "working through and with others to effectively lead and manage the operations of the school, informed by the impact of all decisions on students' learning and needs" (University of Auckland School Leadership Centre, 2006). In this section, it is suggested that evidence of collaborative leadership could include "induction program experiences, seminars, conferences, professional reading, discussion with a mentor or work with a staff member."

The guidance suggests that key principles for reflection include

- Honesty
- Praise where it is due, including for yourself
- Ways in which you would do things differently to achieve a better outcome
- Focus on student learning outcomes
- Your emotional responses, which have an impact on leadership

It also recommends that each reflective entry on the evidence could be written in a different color as a way of showing progress.

Reflection is much more than a few sentences on the results of an activity. A thoughtful reflection is like a dialogue with oneself that creates links between the past, present, and future, and between theory and practice, vision, values, and action. It is an essential element that differentiates an ePortfolio from a simple repository of artifacts. When developing a portfolio, it is necessary to reflect on individual artifacts and their contribution to the portfolio's purpose, but reflective writing can itself be an artifact within a portfolio that demonstrates growth and development. Later, it is important to reflect on what the complete portfolio portrays.

A GUIDE TO REFLECTING

Table 3.3 provides a simple question framework that can help teachers get started with reflection. To use the framework, take an artifact such as a lesson plan, a video clip of a classroom presentation, or a poem written by a group of students, and record something about it in response to each question.

Table 3.3 A Guide to Reflection

Reflection on artifacts can be based on a framework of questions such as these:

- Why did I choose this evidence?
- What was I trying to achieve with this activity?
- How does this fit with my education values?
- How did I feel about the activity?
- How well did I achieve my goals?
- What were the critical factors helping or hindering achievement?
- What have I learned, and what would I do differently next time?
- What are the implications of what I have learned for me, my job, and the teaching profession?

The following selection clearly demonstrates a reflection from one educator's journal, used as an artifact for her teaching portfolio.

When organizing my teaching portfolio, I recognized the need to place "critical reflection" at the forefront. For example, my professional journals have been the life blood of my teaching from the time when I first entered the profession. From one of the pages of my journal I wrote about the most rewarding aspects of teaching:

I am learning that it is often beneficial to be controversial in order to get students to stop believing "on faith" what is taught. I am aware of the great power I wield as a teacher and feel the need to stir and unsettle their sensibilities; to leave them anxious for a time without a safety net. When this is accomplished, it allows students to face their beliefs squarely and come to some kind of resolution. (Latham, personal communication, June 1, 1998)

When extracts from reflective journals are used as artifacts in a portfolio, they help to further develop and explain teachers' professional goals and the activities they have engaged in to achieve these goals. In Chapter 4 we discuss the practical steps that can be followed to develop a complete digital portfolio.

Ten Steps
to Producing
a Digital Portfolio

A portfolio that is truly a story of learning is owned by the learner, structured by the learner, and told in the learner's own voice.

                        ≈ Barrett and Carney (2005)

Once you have amassed a range of artifacts in a personal archive (Step 1), you will be able to produce portfolios for many different purposes. This chapter describes how to prepare a high-quality professional portfolio suitable for digital presentation format. Many of the steps are similar for print-based portfolios. (See Figure 4.1 for a summary of the 10 steps.)

The portfolio development process provides a framework for planning, action, and reflection. The steps that follow are based on the experiences of practicing educators in schools and universities. They have found that producing a portfolio helped to clarify their values, expanded their capacity to reflect on their learning, increased their knowledge and self-esteem, and gave them added confidence in working with colleagues and students. They also found that producing portfolios takes time. But, as Kenneth Wolf states, "Although portfolios can be time consuming to construct and cumbersome to review, they can also capture the complexities of professional practice in ways that no other approach can" (Wolf, 1996a, p. 41).

Developing a portfolio is a process that is personally challenging and, as a result, can lead to enormous personal growth. The journey or process of putting together the portfolio is just as important as the end product. It is important to keep in mind the identity that each portfolio is representing, to keep the individual at the center, and to present with an authentic voice. The 10 steps outlined in this chapter describe this process in more detail.

1. ESTABLISHING A PERSONAL ARCHIVE

As mentioned previously, it is essential to have collected a personal archive to draw on for a professional portfolio. A rich collection, easily accessible, leads to many choices for portfolio development.

2. CLARIFYING AND ARTICULATING VALUES AND VISION

Peter Senge says, quite simply, "Vision . . . is the picture of the future we seek to create" (Senge, 1994, p. 223). Today, both individuals and schools are encouraged to articulate their picture of the future as an inspiration and motivation for

Figure 4.1

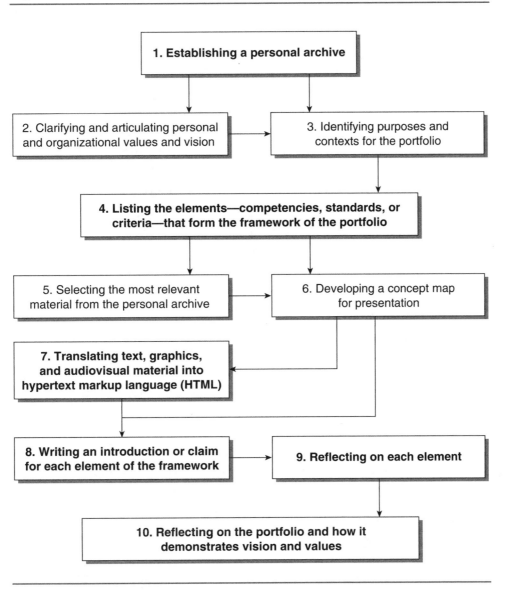

action. Similarly, values and philosophy have been renewed as important underpinnings of the work of individuals and organizations.

An expression of personal beliefs about education, a statement of values underlying one's work, or a vision statement is an excellent way to introduce and focus a portfolio. Sometimes teachers become so caught up in their daily work that they fail to articulate why they are working so hard. As discussed in Chapter 3, a vision statement represents the individual's future intentions and, combined with a statement of purpose, provides the reader with a clear framework for understanding and reviewing the portfolio. The artifacts selected for the portfolio should show how the vision is being realized.

3. ARTICULATING PURPOSE AND CONTEXT

In Chapter 1, we showed the many ways in which portfolios are used to support professional development. There is also a growing movement toward using portfolios to make judgments, such as in a performance review or for hiring purposes. However, the formative type of portfolio, which records development planning, risks taken, successes, and failures, may not be appropriate for review or selection processes, which require a summative assessment. Teachers who have enthusiastically undertaken portfolio development often report that they need a different portfolio for each purpose. Fortunately, a well-organized personal archive makes this possible without too much difficulty.

Most portfolios are specifically designed to communicate with an audience. It is therefore essential to consider the interests, expectations, and experiences of those reading the material. Further consideration of this issue is found in Chapter 6. It is also important to consider how familiar the intended audience is with the material being presented and whether people from other parts of the world will be able to understand what is being portrayed. These considerations will influence the choice and style of language, abbreviations, and terminology. Some terms may have to be explained in detail—even within the same country—to ensure that the desired meaning is conveyed.

4. LISTING THE ELEMENTS THAT FORM THE STRUCTURE

Once the purpose and context are clear, the structure of the portfolio can be planned. For a purpose such as an annual performance review or an application for a specific position, a portfolio can be organized according to the competencies or key skills needed. The development of teacher standards in many states has provided a structure for self-assessment and preparation for professional development, which underpins the portfolio development process. These structural criteria, competencies, and standards are here called elements of the portfolio framework.

In the three examples here, each person has a different purpose (Table 4.1). In some cases, the elements are predetermined, and in others the person developing the portfolio needs to decide which elements to include.

Maria, Jack, and Lee have clearly identified the elements that will form the framework for each of their portfolios, and

Table 4.1 Three Portfolio Structures

Maria: Portfolio to Be Used for Performance Review

Maria is a new principal. She is preparing a portfolio based on the leadership expectations of her state and performance targets she agreed on for the current year with her superintendent (manager). The elements are as follows:

- Lead, coordinate, and facilitate the learning community
- Manage and develop the school culture
- Take responsibility for the school communication networks
- Play a figurehead role in representing the school
- Pursue personal professional development
- Meet performance agreement objectives and goals

Therefore, the evidence she presents in her portfolio for presentation to her superior will need to display outcomes and achievements related to these areas.

Jack: Portfolio to Be Used to Provide Evidence of Meeting Professional Standards

Jack is an experienced classroom teacher. The teacher standards in his state fall into three broad areas: professional knowledge, professional practice, and professional engagement. Within these areas, specific categories include

- Knowledge about learning
- Knowing how to engage students
- A critical understanding of the content
- Respect for students as individuals
- Knowledge of methods, resources, and technologies
- A positive, learning-centered environment
- Monitoring of student progress
- Reflection and critical evaluation of professional effectiveness
- Collaboration with other professionals, parents, and the broader community
- Promotion of the value of education

Jack is developing his portfolio for review with his principal, aiming to show his competence in all of these areas. Therefore, he is using the teacher standards as a basis for collecting material and planning his portfolio.

Lee: Portfolio to Provide Evidence of Professional Development Outcomes

Lee's portfolio is not mandated by her employer. She wants to use the portfolio as a focus for her professional development. After considering her personal goals, she decides that her portfolio for this year will be based on three elements that reflect her current priorities:

- Implementing learning technologies
- Assessment and reporting
- Links with parents

Lee will focus on these three elements when selecting artifacts for inclusion in her portfolio. She intends to include a brief résumé and plans to present the portfolio in an electronic form to show her commitment to learning more about technology.

each will follow his or her framework during portfolio development. The frameworks are developed and brought to life through the selection of artifacts that demonstrate growth and achievement.

5. SELECTING EVIDENCE FROM THE PERSONAL ARCHIVE

Once clear purposes and the elements of the portfolio framework have been chosen, it is time to make a selection from the items of evidence in the personal archive. Quality, not quantity, is the key. Important considerations include the following.

Evidence That Is Recent

Depending on the purpose, there might be guidelines within an organization about how far back in time it is reasonable to go for evidence. Unless the portfolio is designed to show a complete career history, recent evidence is preferable. Although a letter of thanks from 1986 may be a valuable part of a personal archive, it is unlikely to make it into the current portfolio.

A Range of Evidence

A well-rounded portfolio contains artifacts that show action and reflection, curriculum and administrative tasks, work with staff, students, and parents, and individual and team achievements. A selection of text, graphics, sound, and video evidence makes the portfolio interesting for an audience with a range of communication styles and displays different skills. Evidence to cover a range of classroom, whole school, and large-scale activities should be chosen.

Making a Difference

It is particularly helpful to provide evidence of the impact of a teacher's work in the portfolio. This shows the extent to which the activities undertaken in an attempt to achieve the vision have had an effect on the classroom, the school, or a broader audience. This can be shown through survey results, comparative pre-intervention and post-intervention statistics, and feedback from others.

Often there are guidelines about how many artifacts are to be included, but sometimes the developer has to make the decision. Brown and Irby (1995) suggest asking, "What does this piece of evidence add to my portfolio?" When the answer is "nothing," there is no need to include the artifact. On the other hand, Paulson and Paulson (1991) suggest putting in everything that helps to tell the story. The selection of artifacts is a substantial part of the process, but however well organized they are, artifacts do not make a portfolio. The next step involves making connections between them.

6. DEVELOPING A CONCEPT MAP

With the evidence selected, developing a concept map or graphically organizing the evidence assists in the presentation process. It is here that connections between artifacts and elements are highlighted and made specific. The reasons for such links must be identified and expressed simply for the intended audience. A concept map or a storyboard provides a frame of reference for comprehending the portfolio, whether it is in a digital or print form. Figure 4.2 shows an actual concept map drawn by a teacher for her portfolio.

This figure is not complete, but it does show how the material can be arranged, linked, and then reviewed. Any gaps in the material selected or an imbalance between elements should become clear at this point. This step can also provide direction for future professional development or suggest types of evidence that should be collected for the personal archive. Some software programs allow you to select the digital files you need, and the software organizes them according to your desired structure. However, Step 7 shows another way to achieve a similar result.

7. CHOOSING THE APPROPRIATE SOFTWARE

At this stage, there are choices to be made between presentation software, Web authoring, or other tools to create the portfolio. The way all Web authoring programs work is to create the hypertext that allows files to be read and linked on Internet browsers. It is also used to create links within digital documents. Even if the portfolio is not destined for the World Wide Web, it's useful to have the capacity to link files this way on a CD-ROM or DVD. Although you don't need to know about HTML, it enables fine tuning of documents and is of interest to

Figure 4.2   Mapping the Links for a Digital Portfolio

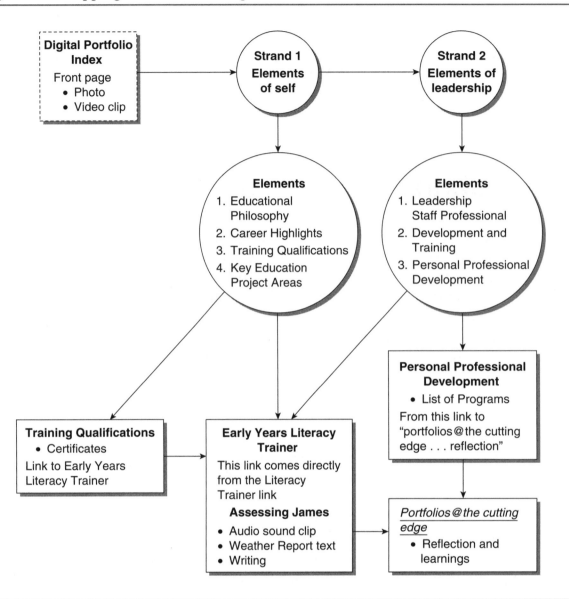

SOURCE: Used with permission of Janette Ellis.

some teachers and students. The example in Figure 4.3 is created in Foliomaker, another kind of software template that does not use HTML.

8. WRITING AN INTRODUCTION FOR EACH ELEMENT

The elements—competencies, standards, or criteria—chosen to make up the framework of the portfolio will need a written

Figure 4.3 Software Template for Linking Portfolio Artifacts

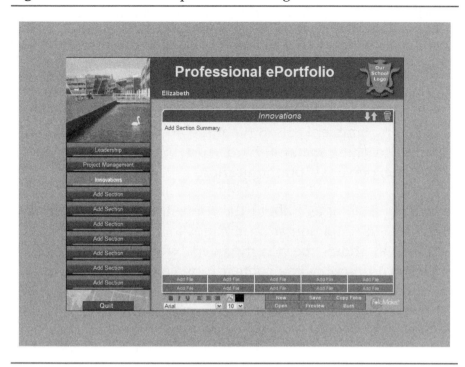

SOURCE: Used with permission of Folios International Pty Ltd. www.foliosinternational.com.

introduction, providing a context for the reader and explaining how the related artifacts demonstrate evidence. In Figure 4.3 the chosen element is Innovations, and the software allows space for this introduction. Following is an introduction in which a teacher explains how the artifacts demonstrate her philosophy of innovation.

> While I love my subject very much, in the "skills vs. content" debate I have always had a leaning in favor of skills. My instinct has always been to seek to equip students to learn for themselves, to integrate their pursuit of a course of English Literature with the development of skills and the self-analytical ability which is fundamental to intellectual independence. In English, it can sometimes be difficult to encourage students to loosen their reliance on secondary critical studies and to develop the self-confidence to assess literary works for themselves. It is a matter of enthusing them about the literature and helping them to find ways of reading the critics critically, distilling useful knowledge, and assessing the critics' arguments against their own perceptions of the evidence of the literary text itself. (Smallwood, 2000, unpublished reflection)

In another example, a claim related to an outcome might include a statement such as this, for the element titled Coping Strategies:

> The evidence I have submitted illustrates my particular approach to coping with the pressures of the job. I am not easily stressed by things that are within my own control: for example, I found planning and writing my first term's teaching material hard work but very satisfying. (Baume, personal communication, 1998)

Making a statement about the context, objectives, and purposes as an introduction or claim helps to make these apparent. Each artifact should be accompanied by a brief statement or caption that describes the context in which it was created and identifying details. The examples in this section demonstrate that this can be done in one or two brief paragraphs. It is not an arduous task.

9. REFLECTING ON ARTIFACTS AND ELEMENTS

Reflection, as described in Chapter 3, is a very important part of the learning process. Therefore, it should be an aspect of every portfolio. Reflective commentaries do more than describe the artifacts and their context; they examine the knowledge, skills, attitudes, and values of the portfolio developer.

In the following example, a teacher reflects on her role in the school's self-review process:

> Although I have provided leadership in a range of areas including managing projects, curriculum development and staff welfare matters, this artifact represents my most recent and in some ways most challenging role in that I had to draw on a range of communications skills (to persuade, cajole, resolve conflict, gain consensus), analytical skills to interpret and comment about the data gathered during the process, and project management skills to develop and meet timelines.
>
> On reflection, I would have preferred for staff to have more time to analyze the data rather than to discuss an analysis I presented to them. This would have encouraged deeper debate and discussion of educational issues

than did occur. The Principal agreed to allocate more time to charter development at staff meetings and Professional Development meetings and we had a longer timeline so I was able to provide more time for debate when we moved into the phase of new charter development. Additional personal Professional Development I undertook in communication skills also gave me some additional tools to use to encourage staff input and I am now confident the quality of the new charter will reflect the more active input of staff, Council and students and thus be more representative of a collective view. (Taylor, 1997, unpublished reflection)

This example demonstrates the ways in which the teacher works as a leader in her school and what she has learned from the review process. The inclusion of reflective writing provides more than a catalog of achievements: It provides rich information about the teacher's values and goals.

10. REFLECTING ON THE PORTFOLIO AS A WHOLE

Although this step is last in the list, it is the key to the ongoing nature of the portfolio approach, as the growth demonstrated and the achievements highlighted are now reconsidered. Reflection helps make portfolio production a recursive process.

Mary Diez (1996) reminds us that the portfolio encourages reflection in at least three different ways. It provides the freedom and discipline to identify a structure that views or presents one's own work, provides the opportunity to assess one's strengths and weaknesses by careful examination of the artifacts used to meet the specified framework, and leads to professional goal setting for the future through self-assessment and reflection. Chapter 3 discussed some ways of reflecting on artifacts, and at this point it is possible to reflect on the complete portfolio. This reflection can take the form of an essay that is also placed in the personal archive, to be referred to in a later portfolio as a means of showing professional growth. Reflection on a complete portfolio should focus on its purpose, the values and vision it represents, the professional growth it outlines, and the rubrics against which it might be evaluated. The following example is a concluding reflection to a principal's portfolio in which she provides evidence of her professional growth and leadership:

We have made many changes, both to curriculum, to the way we do things and to the manner in which we work together. Staff has experienced a "mindset" change. They now understand why we must walk our talk, why quality is important all the time without question, why lifelong learning is honored through professional development opportunities, why we must share our learning if we are to be a true learning community, and why we look upon everything through our "systems" eyes. We are not just a part of some thing, we are a "whole." People now understand the complexities of the decisions we make, how one small change affects many other areas of our lives. Now people look for the many different points of view, the many results that we will have due to the changes we make. Our staff now see things in "big picture" mode. What a wonderful experience! And what a challenge this was. (McLean, unpublished reflection, 1998, p. 6)

Reflection is both something that teachers should learn to do competently and a means to achieve other goals as well. This type of reflection can help the audience understand what the teacher has learned from the development process and how she plans to implement what she has learned in her work. Reflection is a more central means of learning for experienced practitioners than it is for novices, suggests McIntyre (1993). Although learning to reflect is very important for preservice teachers, he argues, it is probably more useful as a means to learning for experienced teachers, who have greater experience to bring to bear. They can use their reflections to move from consideration of goals, to consequences, values, and assumptions, and finally to consider social, ethical, and political issues.

These steps form the basis of the portfolio development process. Now that the content is complete, the portfolio should be saved for storage on a CD-ROM, DVD, thumb drive, computer hard drive, or Web server. But without continual reflection on vision and values, updates of the personal archive, and awareness of new purposes and contexts, portfolio development could become just another production line. The purpose determined at the outset indicates who the audience will be, and the format of the portfolio should be appropriate for that audience. In Chapter 5 we look at some of the technologies that help in their creation, and in Chapter 6 we return to methods of communicating with a range of audiences through digital portfolios.

Understanding the Technology

Keeping the Portfolio Alive

Tell me and I'll forget; show me and I may remember;
involve me and I'll understand.

ஒ Chinese proverb

With the advent of software tools designed to simplify the process of portfolio development, there are two very important things to remember. The material in your archive must be updated frequently, and the selections you make for each portfolio must be tailored to the purpose and audience. Otherwise you will have a static, not living, portfolio.

Baron (1996) describes the technical aspects of producing a digital portfolio for visual artists, designed particularly as a marketing tool. These methods easily apply to educators who want to record and present information in digital form, and the basic steps are described in this chapter. Contrary to what many believe, it is possible to produce simple, attractive documents without the latest high-tech equipment, using commonly available software. The women@thecuttingedge program (Hartnell-Young & Morriss, 1999) specifically set out to work with teachers to increase their self-knowledge and technology skills through development of a purposeful portfolio. A summary of the content of the program and the rationale for these activities are shown in Table 5.1.

HARDWARE USED IN CREATING DIGITAL PORTFOLIOS

Many of the useful and commonly found hardware items are listed in Table 5.2, followed by some technical tips for preparing material for a digital portfolio.

If any artifacts are not yet in digital form, they must be transferred into a digital format. It is very helpful to choose a system of consistent and logical file names for the archive. Some teachers use a consistent prefix for each file relating to a particular element, such as leadership. The name of each file relating to this element might then begin with the letters "l-e-a-d." Once production has started, it becomes very time-consuming to change file names because all the links to a page in the portfolio must be changed if the name of the file in which it is found is changed.

It is important to keep the size of individual graphic files to a minimum. Sites with fancy graphics can take a long time to download. You cannot be certain that the audience will have access to technology that is as efficient as yours is. Download time from the Internet is 2 seconds per graphic plus 1 second

Table 5.1   Content of the Cutting Edge Professional Development
Program (Hartnell-Young & Morriss, 1999)

Topic	Purpose
What is a professional portfolio?	To inform about purposes, form, content, and presentation of portfolios
Sample multimedia portfolios (demonstrated by local teachers)	To show examples of structure and content and demonstrate that multimedia can be created by ordinary teachers
Multimedia skill audit (self-administered)	To establish baseline data regarding technology skills
Research on the Internet about portfolios	To familiarize with Internet search engines and evaluate preparatory work by sharing sites found by participants before the program
Evaluating digital multimedia design	To engage with and review multimedia portfolios and develop criteria for good communication
Collecting and storing material for a personal archive	To discuss and establish systems for organizing evidence, including digital files
Planning a purposeful portfolio structure using criteria	To demonstrate and use the concept of a site map for multimedia, including links
Producing the first page (and subsequent pages)	To experience hands-on creation of HTML and inserting images
Creating links	To practice creating hypertext links between the pages produced earlier
Using equipment (e.g., scanner, digital camera, sound and video recorders, CD writers)	To produce a range of actual files to incorporate into the portfolio
Reflective writing	To practice the discipline of reflection and create material for the portfolio
Presenting a digital portfolio	To upload to the Internet and introduce a portfolio into an interview or presentation

Table 5.2   Common Hardware and Its Uses

Hardware and Equipment	Uses
Computer (desktop or laptop)	Too numerous to list
Camera	Photographs activities, documents, buildings, etc.
Digital camera and camera phone	Stores photographs directly in digital form
Scanner	Converts printed documents and images to digital form
Modem (internal or external to computer)	Forms connections to network for Internet access
Video camera	Records moving images
Sound recorder	Records sound
Computer with sound card and internal or external microphone	Records sound in digital format
Computer with video adapter card and capture software	Plays video recordings on computer
CD writer	Stores large amounts of material on CD-ROMs
Computer with CD or DVD reader	Reads CD-ROM or DVD
Memory stick	Stores digital files
iPod	Stores and plays digital files
Data projector	Connects to computer to display images or text on a large screen

per kilobyte, so a 30-K graphic would take 32 seconds to download under average conditions. 50 K is thought to be the maximum size for this type of use if you want to keep your audience's attention. One minute can seem like a very long time to wait for information to be downloaded from the Internet.

Software for concept mapping and other graphic organizing tools is available, and teachers find it helpful for more than just portfolio development. Most of the examples used in this book show portfolios that teachers have created by devising their own structures. They then used Web authoring software or simple templates to complete the portfolio. When planning your digital portfolio, it is wise to begin with the structure of the end product in mind.

It is important to think of the audience in terms of design as well as content. Customized portfolio software usually provides fewer options for creative portfolio developers. Presentation and Web authoring software provides simple ways to modify the appearance and color scheme of documents. The important thing is simply to develop a portfolio that communicates, avoiding gimmicks and using appropriate font sizes, clear color schemes, and navigation prompts.

Don't forget to save your work frequently and back up your files. Make sure your archive and any portfolios in progress are saved in more than one place. Losing your work is extremely frustrating.

SOFTWARE FOR ePORTFOLIOS

Some of the most readily available tools are off-the-shelf authoring tools. These include presentation or slide show tools, such as Microsoft PowerPoint, and Web authoring software such as Microsoft FrontPage, Macromedia Dreamweaver, and Netscape Composer.

A specific tool for simple portfolio development is Foliomaker, illustrated in Figure 5.1 and available from www .foliosinternational.com. More complex customized portfolio authoring systems often rely on databases, where the artifacts are stored. They are then able to be retrieved for a range of digital portfolios. Such products include Concord Masterfile, Nuventive iWebfolio, and Folio by ePortaro. These also allow aggregation of assessment data for use by the school or other institution. This type of software is also available from open-source developers such as Open Source Portfolio Initiative (OSPI, http://www.osportfolio.org).

GETTING STARTED

A simple way to get started is to use a template, such as that shown in Figure 5.1. On the left side are the "Add Section" buttons, which can be given the headings of the desired portfolio structure, and the "Add File" buttons at the bottom create links to specific artifacts on the computer. This software program

Figure 5.1   A Simple Commercial Portfolio Template

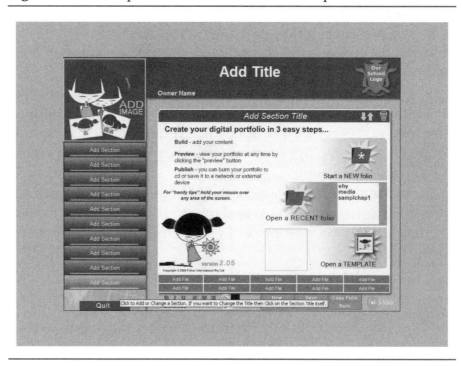

SOURCE: Used with permission of Folios International Pty Ltd. www.foliosinternational.com.

Figure 5.2   A Web-Based Template for School Leaders

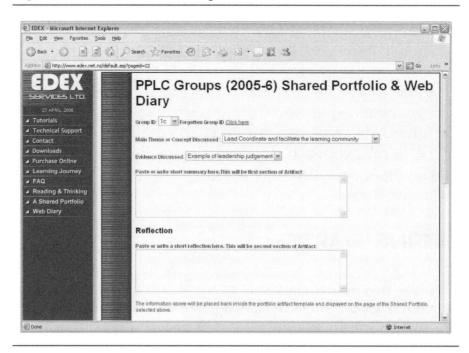

SOURCE: Used with permission of David Stewart.

creates portfolios saved to the computer, CD-ROM, or memory stick rather than Web-based portfolios.

A second simple, perhaps more creative way to get started is to use presentation software such as Microsoft PowerPoint, as in Figure 2.1 in Chapter 2. In this case, the structure can be displayed on the first slide, and links can be created to pages further on in the presentation or items stored separately, such as pages on the Web. Although this method can be quite satisfactory, it generally results in a linear portfolio presentation.

A portfolio on the Web can also be created through a template, as in the New Zealand example mentioned previously. Figure 5.2 shows a text-based template.

Another way to create a portfolio is to use off-the-shelf Web authoring software without portfolio templates, as in the following example created by Elizabeth.

Elizabeth started her portfolio by collecting material about an industry placement she took as part of her professional development. This experience enabled her to learn more about the culture of a large multinational company. Her personal archive consists of evidence of the work she did in the company, including a photo taken with managers after the presentation of a report she wrote, a summary of the report, reflection on what she learned, and several papers she wrote after the experience. She selected these as the best artifacts from a much larger collection. The photograph is a JPEG file, and the documents are all in Microsoft Word or PDF files. This means that all of Elizabeth's documents are now in a digital format.

Figure 5.3 is a flowchart Elizabeth designed to illustrate how she wanted to link the material. Elizabeth created the pages to be short and informative and decided to use only one photograph to allow easy loading for most Internet browsers. On each page, she decided to include a button that links back to the first page in the section, and she also included a link to a Web site where one of her papers was published. Finally, to make sure that her readers would be able to contact her for further information or to ask questions, she designed a link that included her e-mail address.

Once the links had been designed, the front page, or introduction, could be written. Using a Web authoring program, Elizabeth wrote her introduction and saved it as the index. This will signal to a Web browser that this is the home page of the portfolio. This page can then be linked to other documents, including the "Professional Development" element in the following section.

Figure 5.3   Designing Links for Hypertext

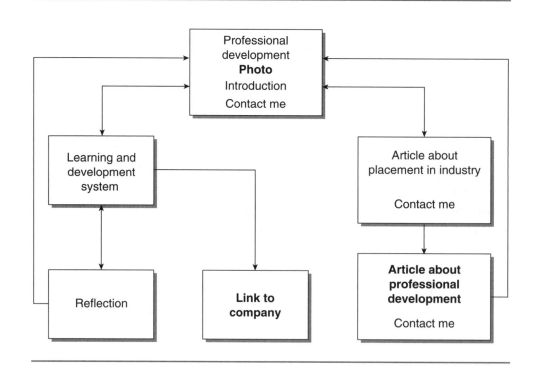

Elizabeth used Web authoring software to prepare this section for her portfolio. She began by creating a new document (under the File menu). In order to keep the page neat and well spaced, Elizabeth used a table layout command to create a table with two columns and two rows. She then typed the heading "Professional Development" in the left-hand column. She used the Insert menu to locate the JPEG file with the scanned image of her photograph, which she then inserted into the page. The image was only 26 K, so she knew it would not take her readers too long to load. The text accompanying the photo was copied from a word-processed document and pasted into the Web editor. Figure 5.4 shows the resulting portfolio page. Here the underlined text ("Learning and Development System Executive Summary") is linked to other another document in her portfolio, as described in the next section.

LINKING DOCUMENTS AND SITES

The capacity to provide links between documents is one of the major attractions of a digital portfolio. In many off-the-shelf programs, one can create links quite easily by selecting the text

Figure 5.4 A Linked Page From Elizabeth's Portfolio

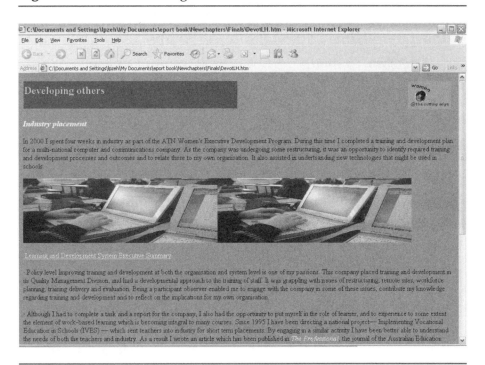

on the page to be linked (such as "Learning and Development System Executive Summary"), choosing the Insert menu, and then clicking on the Hyperlink command. You can then browse to find the file you want to link to. Text and images can also be linked to a specific location in the document, such as text, an image, or a video clip.

Whatever choice is made, a click on Insert will create the links between documents. The linked text will change color and will be underlined, indicating that it is linked to further information in the same document, to another file in the portfolio, or even to a document on another Web site. Follow the same steps to link images, video, or audio to text and to link to other Web sites.

The only way to see the complete document is to scroll down the page, using the arrow on the right side of the screen. However, the first link, shown here in underlined text, will be apparent. The link is activated by clicking on the words "Learning and Development System Executive Summary," which have been highlighted and appear in a different color.

Figure 5.5 shows the layout (including links) that Elizabeth developed after creating and compiling her chosen elements. This is just one example of providing links within an element. You can apply the same procedures to the other elements.

Figure 5.5   Contents of a Linked Element in a Digital Portfolio

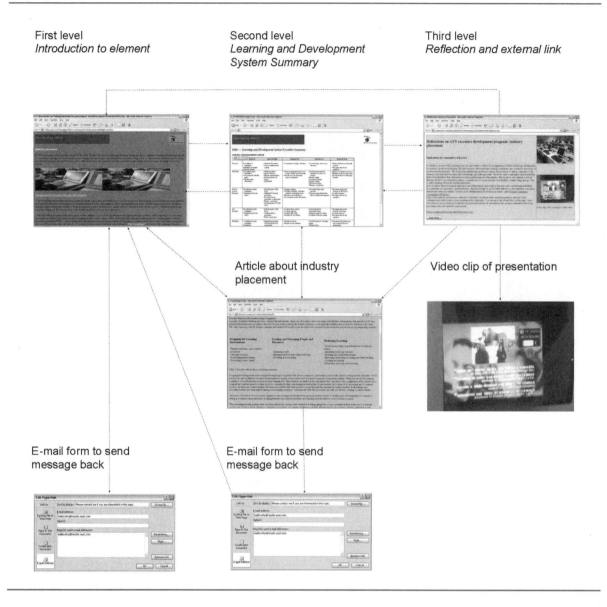

- *Providing navigation symbols.* One of the most important links is the text, icon, or button that takes the reader back to the home page or to preceding documents. Without links back, the reader can get lost. On each page, there should be an indicator telling the reader how to move on and how to return to the home page. These links are created as described earlier. Clear and consistent buttons or symbols, such as forward and backward arrows, should be provided to guide the reader. These can be created in Web authoring software, downloaded from one of the free graphic sites on the Internet, or designed individually using drawing software. Each symbol is an image file (such as a GIF or JPEG file) and can be inserted into a document and linked in the same way as other links. For example, a back arrow placed at the end of a page might then be linked to the first page, or home page, in your portfolio.

- *Creating links to other relevant sites.* Sometimes a portfolio makes reference to work that has been commercially published, to previous employers, or to schools that have their own Web sites. In such cases, it can be useful to provide links to specific areas of other relevant sites. This is not difficult and can be done by following the Insert and Link commands previously described. However, it may be necessary to seek permission from the managers of the Web sites you plan to link to.

It is important to remember that although other sites have a great deal of interesting information, they may not have a way of linking back to the original portfolio. This means the reader who follows these links could become lost and never get back to the original portfolio.

OWNERSHIP AND COPYRIGHT ISSUES

The wide availability of material on the Web and the ability to copy text from Web documents raises the important issue of copyrights. The author of the original work usually is the copyright holder. Copyright laws indicate that any original work is protected even if there is no notice to this effect in the document. It is a good idea to place a short copyright notice on each document you use in your portfolio. The copyright laws cover digital forms such as text, photographs, and audio files. If a photograph contains images of others, such as students, parents, or colleagues, a model release—a signed permission document—is required from each person shown in the image.

Portfolio developers need to be aware of the copyright laws and to err on the side of caution. Some sites contain public domain materials, such as graphics, that can be incorporated freely into new sites. However, as with any publication, it is always important to check the source of the material and verify that the material is indeed in the public domain.

CUSTOMIZED OR OFF THE SHELF?

Using the most fully developed customized systems or traditional authoring tools reduces the cognitive load for teachers but deprives them of an excellent opportunity to develop their technology skills. Many companies allow the downloading of trial versions of portfolio software from their Web sites, so you can try several. A Google search will identify plenty to choose from.

Once you have created a digital portfolio, it is time to review it with colleagues or present it to your intended audience. Chapter 6 looks at this aspect of portfolio development.

Presenting a Digital Portfolio

A personal story of learning shared with an invited audience: a digital theatre: by invitation only!

∽ Sutherland (personal communication, 2006)

Representation of identity, or perhaps more accurately multiple identities, is enabled through portfolio development. Cope and Kalantzis (2000) claim that maintaining rich and diverse identities is essential and that presenting self and culture across a range of media are central skills in the new economy. The choices we make in the process of creating portfolios are key to our ability to create self-identity (Giddens, 1991). Whatever the extent of these choices, a person engages in what Giddens calls the reflexive project of the self. Digital portfolios have a part to play in the project, with their focus on the individual's life achievement and personal reflection, particularly where they allow choices to be made in purpose, content, and presentation format.

Portfolio presentation implies an audience and therefore is a communication between presenter and audience. When portfolios look outward, they embrace the 21st-century literacies, including understanding of audience and society. Pachler (2001) reminds us that creating and distributing our own work makes us active participants in creating culture, but we also need skills, such as informatic, visual, and critical media literacies. These skills are a critical area of teachers' work in the 21st century, providing an intrinsic benefit and enabling us all to engage in dialogue with software producers and distributors who devise ePortfolio solutions. By presenting portfolios to various audiences, teachers learn the skills they need to develop with their students. This chapter describes several ways to present digital portfolios.

CONSIDERING YOUR AUDIENCE

As discussed in previous chapters, the purpose of the portfolio determines both its audience and its structure. The audience might include

- Colleagues
- Students
- Supervisors
- A school community
- A selection panel in another school or organization
- Award-granting or accreditation agencies

- Prospective employers around the world
- Unknown Internet surfers

An important aspect of 21st-century literacy is consideration of the audience's languages, culture, and experience with technology. Once you know the nature of the audience, it is important to find out whether they are prepared for the type of portfolio you plan to produce. For example, will they be able to read a DVD or CD-ROM or access the Internet? If they have Internet access, what is their technical capacity for viewing images, for example? A living portfolio can be easily modified by the author and easily read by the audience. Digital multimedia technology allows this type of flexibility, and the level of sophistication used is determined in part by the audience's capacity to access the technology. Once you have determined the necessary information about the audience, you can decide which format to use for portfolio presentation.

Throughout this book, we have emphasized the distinction between an archive, containing a wide range of artifacts, and a portfolio, which is a purposeful selection, with accompanying reflection. In general terms, the archive can be stored locally, such as on a personal computer, in personal folder space on a local area network (as in a school setting), or on a centralized Web server that hosts the work of many people. Where the archive is stored usually is of no concern to the audience, but how they can access various digital portfolios certainly is.

TRANSPORTABILITY

Because portfolios are traditionally portable, they can be saved on a personal memory stick, iPod, or laptop computer. These portfolios are completely in the control of the producer, who decides when they can be opened. The memory stick must be connected to a computer, which may be provided by the audience or the presenter. Small screens of mobile devices can be a problem when one is presenting a professional portfolio. For presentation to very small groups, the laptop screen may be sufficient, and for larger groups the presentation can be shown via a data projector attached to the computer, with the image projected onto a large screen. Laptop computers can be transported easily to conferences, meetings, and interviews.

Figure 6.1 CD Portfolio Used as a Business Card

Multiple copies of portfolios can be stored on CD-ROMs or DVDs. The two types of blank CDs for recording are rewritable CDs (CD-RW) and recordable CDs (CD-R). The latter can be written only once, whereas the former (CD-RW) can be reused. Most new computers sold today contain CD-ROM drives that are able to burn and read CD-ROMs, and increasingly, computers are able to read and burn DVDs. Some portfolios are saved to business-card sized CD-ROMs and handed out instead of the paper cards (Figure 6.1).

Access to this type of hardware is becoming more widespread for both the portfolio producer and the audience. However, remember to check in advance that your audience is able to view a CD-ROM or DVD if you plan to send your portfolio in this format.

PUBLIC PRESENTATION OF YOUR PORTFOLIO

Presentation can significantly increase the impact of a message. However, referring to a portfolio in a situation such as an interview takes some preparation and rehearsal. The audience should be made aware of the existence of the portfolio in advance so they are not surprised by this type of presentation. When using a laptop computer for presentation, make sure the portfolio presentation is set up in advance. The computer should not be a distraction to the presenter or the panel but rather a natural adjunct to the information verbally presented. It is helpful to rehearse a pathway through your digital portfolio.

For a real-time presentation to an audience to be effective, these points should be kept in mind:

- The equipment must be prepared and tested before presentation time.
- The audience should be able to see the screen clearly.
- The presenter should appear confident with the technology.
- The presenter must maintain eye contact with the audience.
- Multimedia material must support what the presenter says.

WEB ACCESS

Creating a portfolio for distribution on the Internet is similar to creating a CD-ROM or DVD, but the audience is wider, and they can access your portfolio at any time. There are various ways in which the producer can control which material is made publicly available. Many of the database systems on the market today enable the producer to set levels of access so that only selected audiences can read the portfolio or specific items via the Web. It is also possible to load the portfolio onto a server and maintain some control over access by giving out the Web address or URL only to selected audiences.

When communicating with the audience, the portfolio producer also needs to remember that various Web browsers are used to access the Internet. This means that the same document can appear differently to individual users. Even on the same browser, users can change the preference settings for font, text size, and color, so it is difficult to predict how the pages will be seen, although the basic information certainly will be displayed. The size of the window can also be adjusted, so the layout of the pages can also appear differently. It is therefore useful to test the portfolio on various computers to see how it appears. To avoid difficulties, keep the design simple.

VERIFICATION

As with other forms of digital and Web-based data, there is growing concern among some audiences about how to verify the authenticity of portfolio artifacts. Have they really been created by the owner of the portfolio? Technological solutions to this question are being developed:

> Those that view the portfolio, prospective employers, admission officers, etc., need to know that the portfolio they have been granted access to is genuine so that they can make hiring and admission decisions based on it. The IMS Digital Repositories group, as well as other digital signature methods, will ensure this; however, it will require ongoing work via trial and deployment to develop best practices. (eport.consortium.org, 2003)

When teachers are working collaboratively, the question of who created the material is less relevant if judgments of worth can also occur in a collaborative context. Similarly, when portfolio authoring is a coached activity, it is difficult to isolate the individual inputs. The National Board for Professional Teaching Standards portfolio was deliberately structured to promote this kind of teamwork (Carney, 2004), as was the original model for women@thecuttingedge (Hartnell-Young & Morriss, 1999).

We believe that the most effective way to judge the veracity of artifacts and claims is to consider the individual, or collegiate, voice. This means that the slickest portfolios, or those based on rigid templates, might be less useful in establishing authenticity than those that are clearly created by an amateur. A heartfelt comment about the extent of professional growth, or some corny design aspects, might signal that this is truly the work of the claimant.

SECURITY AND PRIVACY

Many schools have policies to guide teachers and students regarding the posting of personal information on the Web. Yet it is still possible to find digital portfolios with personal photographs, home addresses, and telephone numbers. Although it is lovely to share with a worldwide audience, experience has shown that schools must take great care with such information, and portfolio developers must also take privacy and security into account. You must obtain permission to use photographs that include other people, and it might be appropriate not to label them with names at all.

Once your portfolio is finished, it is time to evaluate how well it meets its purpose and communicates its message. Chapter 7 contains useful information about ways to do this.

Evaluating a Digital Portfolio

The assessment of a portfolio is inextricably related to its purpose, content and structure.

༄ Baume (2001, p. 5)

We have described portfolio development as a process of professional growth that focuses on the individual at the center. Evaluation of professional growth must reflect the person and be assisted, not hindered, by the presentation of the portfolio. Formative evaluation takes place in a continuous process during the development of a portfolio, whereas summative evaluation occurs at one point in time, after completion of a portfolio. Making judgments about professional portfolios is perhaps the most problematic issue in the process.

Barrett and Carney (2005) suggest that some of the purposes described in Chapter 1 actually are in competition with each other, leading to confusion. However, the growing importance of feedback in professional growth, itself a form of judgment, suggests that there is a continuum of evaluative judgment that can be used in relation to portfolios, from self-evaluation to high-stakes assessment. This chapter provides suggestions for self-managed portfolio evaluation and rubrics that developers, supervisors, appraisers, or selection panels can use to evaluate portfolios.

Green and Smyser (1996) link the teacher's portfolio closely to education reform, arguing that many reform programs fail because they do not recognize that fundamental change in education does not occur without renewal and professional development of teachers. This approach entails a change in how teaching is assessed and how professional growth is guided. It is in this context that the focus must be on the purpose of portfolio development, remembering that it is a vehicle for individual growth that has the additional benefit of acting as a record for communication to others.

Questions are often asked, such as Who should judge the portfolio? What aspects of the portfolio are most important to consider during any assessment? How will audiences judge the value of a portfolio? It is important to clarify what is being evaluated: Is it the portfolio as a digital entity? Is it judging the person represented in the portfolio? Is it the fit between the representation of the person and a set of criteria or a specific job?

EVALUATION TO SUPPORT LEARNING

In this book, we have argued that the development of the portfolio is not an end but a means to an end. The outcome is improved teacher and student learning. In this chapter, we tackle evaluation: identifying the value inherent in the portfolio. Some of the quotes we have gathered use the term *assessment* in a way that includes our understanding of the term *evaluation*; we use both terms here.

Wolf (1994, p. 132) suggests that portfolio evaluators must possess sophisticated skills. They should be "individuals who (1) are very knowledgeable and experienced in the content, context and grade level being assessed, (2) represent a diversity of perspectives and backgrounds, and (3) are trained in the criteria and procedures for scoring the portfolio." These valuable attributes seem to reside in the producer and his or her peers. Therefore, for professional growth, it is important that the evaluation of all portfolios begins with the creator.

The portfolio producer first reflects on the selection and presentation of material, to decide whether it meets the stated purpose, and on the extent to which the resulting portfolio truly represents and reflects the significance of his or her work. It is tempting to be dazzled by the presentation to the detriment of the content. A portfolio designed to document professional growth should include artifacts displaying evidence consistent with one's purpose, values, and philosophy and reflection on the evidence and on the learning and development displayed in the portfolio. Reflecting on the process can also include considering the technological skill development that occurred along the way and how this type of new knowledge can be shared with students and other teachers. In this case, the portfolio acts as a videotape rather than a snapshot.

TOOLS TO ASSIST EVALUATION

Rubrics often are developed by teachers, professional associations, or educational administrators to assist evaluation. Green and Smyser (1996) suggest that when portfolios are used to evaluate teachers, the rubrics should be developed in collaboration with the teachers themselves, and Brown and Irby (1997) report that this has occurred in various school districts. Rubrics are not to be used only after completion of a portfolio; they provide a checklist to consult while developing the portfolio. Table 7.1 contains generally applicable rubric guidelines that focus on the contents of a portfolio and can be used by both producers and audiences.

Table 7.1   Rubrics for Portfolio Evaluation

	Excellent	*Satisfactory*	*Unsatisfactory*
Statement of purpose, philosophy, and values	Clearly describes purpose of the portfolio and the educational philosophy of the producer.	Describes purpose of the portfolio and the educational philosophy of the producer.	Not stated or unclear.
Framework matching purpose (e.g., selection criteria, competency standards)	Elements clearly identified and appropriate links made.	Elements identified.	The framework is not listed, does not match purpose, or is not clear.
Suitable evidence for each criterion	Clear links made between evidence and element.	Evidence available for each element.	Evidence not related to the elements.
Evidence consistent with underlying values	Links between evidence and underlying values are clearly expressed and demonstrated; shows the values in action.	Evidence is congruent with the expressed educational philosophy and values.	No link between evidence and underlying values.
Evidence of a range of scales	Links made between evidence from classroom, schoolwide, and professional activities.	Evidence chosen from classroom, schoolwide, and professional activities.	Range not evident (e.g., relies on classroom evidence only).
Evidence shows change over time, progress toward achievement of goals	Explicit evidence of progress toward goals, clearly articulated through reflection and synthesis.	Timeframe indicated, little stated evidence of growth.	No time period or progress indicated.
Various types of evidence to ensure reliability	Wide range of text, graphics, photographs, sound, video, and other types of	More than one type of evidence (e.g., text plus photographs, or text plus video).	Only one type of evidence.

(Continued)

Table 7.1 (Continued)

	Excellent	*Satisfactory*	*Unsatisfactory*
	evidence to meet the multiple intelligences; student work, feedback.		
Appropriate amount of evidence	Reflection illuminates the evidence.	Each piece of evidence provides new information.	Too little evidence or repetition of evidence.
Reflection on artifacts linking theory and practice	Clearly argued statement reflecting broad understanding of theory and practice.	Statement identifying practices that reflect relevant educational theory.	No theoretical underpinning expressed.
Reflection on the overall portfolio	Statement links back to the philosophy of teaching and how the portfolio meets intended purpose.	Reflective statement and brief review of intended purpose.	No statement of overall reflection.
Individual voice	Overall language, content, and style reveal personality.	Voice shows through from time to time.	Generic language and style cloud individual voice.

Another useful rubric is provided by the International Society for Technology in Education (ISTE) in the form of a sample rubric for a multimedia presentation or project, available on the Web at http://cnets.iste.org. It considers aspects such as organization of content, subject matter knowledge, copyright and documentation, and graphic design, all areas of relevance to a professional portfolio. The very simple checklist in Table 7.2 also provides some guidelines to use before publishing a digital portfolio. Some of the main aspects of development that can affect the communication of material are covered.

Consulting this checklist can help you make sure your portfolio is set up properly and in an organized manner, which will enable the audience to access it easily.

Table 7.2   Checklist for Developers and Audience for a Digital Portfolio

Ask	Yes	No	N/A
Is the design clear?			
Is the text easy to read throughout the portfolio?			
Do the graphics load quickly?			
Are the graphics supported by text?			
Is navigation easy?			
Are the links obvious to the reader?			
Do the links lead to further information and lead back (no dead ends)?			
Is the use of color attractive?			
Is there a consistent style throughout?			
Are sound and video files clear and informative?			
Are sound and video labeled and supported by text?			
Are there contact details for the developer?			
Is copyright acknowledged appropriately?			
Is there a clear indication of production dates for the portfolio?			
If the portfolio has been updated, is there information related to the updates?			

AUDIENCE EVALUATION

As noted earlier, the continuum of evaluation includes feedback from peers and other professionals. Some portfolio systems are designed to capture this feedback in an ongoing way. The New Zealand First-Time Principals portfolio encourages this process:

> Each person constructing their portfolio uploads selected files to the site, hyperlinks them to the particular portfolio template, and then includes reflection and comment. They make independent decisions about reviewers and, if this feature is activated, reviewers can also add to the reflective comment. As this is a Web application, participants can access their portfolio through password-protected browser contact. (Stewart, personal communication, 2006)

This process recognizes the importance of continual feedback, adjustment, and reflection in personal development. Whether it is feedback on individual elements of a portfolio or on the whole story being told, another perspective on the material is important. Reflecting on how an audience responded to a portfolio will help you present subsequent versions.

Those who view and evaluate ePortfolios need the skills of critical literacy just as much as their creators do. When a portfolio is being evaluated by someone other than the developer, it is important that the evaluator acknowledge the experience and position of its creator. For instance, the expectations for a principal's portfolio would be more complex than those for a first-year teacher, although the areas of evaluation could be the same.

It is wise to address all aspects of the personal evaluation described in Table 7.1 before presenting the portfolio to an evaluator. This way, you are making sure you present the best possible portfolio you can produce. Evaluators look for awareness of the teaching context and position and a good fit between the structure of the portfolio and its purpose. They also look for evidence that shows personal values and the unique contributions you have made. The complete package of a digital portfolio can show an employer that you are innovative and aware of information technology and its uses.

Audiences often have their own understanding of purposes, and little work has been done to ascertain whether they have the time or the interest to view portfolios. In schools there might appear to be little time available to consider portfolios. If it is a valuable activity, however, schools will find a way to incorporate portfolio development and feedback into regular activities. Outside schools, employers are seen as a large potential audience. Although it is believed that they will value ePortfolios (Love, McKean, & Gathercoal, 2004), a recent Australian research study (Leece, 2005) found that only 10% of employers had heard of portfolios, and 28% would consider using them for recruitment.

ASSESSING LEARNING THROUGH PORTFOLIO DEVELOPMENT

A fundamental principle of this book is that educators grow professionally while producing digital portfolios. They become producers as well as consumers of technology, enabling them to become more confident about using it in their daily work. They learn more about using the World Wide Web for teaching, research, and communication with a global audience. This transfer of knowledge and skills will benefit not only them but their students, colleagues, and community. But more fundamentally, educators can show evidence of their deep learning, as Baume, Yorke, and Coffey note:

> Portfolios have two valuable components for the assessment of professional abilities. First, they contain naturally occurring, authentic evidence of the work of a professional. They thus have at least the potential to be highly valid, offering primary evidence of outcomes achieved rather than secondary evidence such as the ability to talk about how outcomes could be achieved. Second, they involve critical commentary, in which the candidate reflects on the evidence he or she has presented and makes a claim that this evidence shows how they have attained the intended outcomes of the course, and "further" have done so in a way that is demonstrably underpinned by required professional values. (Baume, Yorke, & Coffey, 2004, p. 452)

At present, we rely on the reports of people involved in portfolio development to identity the learning that takes place rather than measuring the effect of portfolios directly. In the future, this learning might be measured in other ways. Wilkerson and Lang (2003) point out that when portfolios are used for certification or other high-stakes decision making, they must be psychometrically sound, or they may be subject to a host of legal challenges.

Carney (2004) rightly raises questions about whether portfolios can be assessed reliably and, if so, whether they then enable valid interpretations about achievement. Furthermore, she suggests that even if this is possible, using portfolios in high-stakes decisions might destroy their usefulness as a learning tool. The debate about whether portfolios should be used only for professional learning and never for assessment is likely to continue for some time.

It is clear that this is an area for more consideration, and teachers embarking on and experienced in portfolio development are well placed to contribute to these discussions. In Chapter 8, we look at ways in which people interested in digital portfolios can share their knowledge and influence future developments.

Sharing the Knowledge

Global Networking

The depth and range of our colleagues' experience, skills and achievements haven't really surprised me, but seeing them on screen and celebrating them together has been more powerful than I might have imagined.

 ❧ Pearce (personal communication, 1999)

One of the important aspects of digital portfolio development is the capacity for connecting with others to build knowledge. Scardamalia and Bereiter (1999) argue that where a collaborative knowledge-building approach is adopted, the work of schools is the construction of collective knowledge. This means that teachers and students are participants in a learning organization, often working in one or many communities of practice (Wenger, 1998). A community of practice is a group of people who share a concern, a set of problems, or a passion about a topic and who deepen their knowledge and expertise in this area by interacting on an ongoing basis (Wenger, McDermott, & Snyder, 2002). The definition in itself is not new, but as Wenger et al. argue, a focus on intentional and systematic knowledge management has become increasingly important in the knowledge economy, and communities of practice are seen to be important in the life of educational organizations.

Among other things, Wenger suggests that any learning community must push its boundaries and interact with other communities of practice in a purposeful way. It is therefore deep and wide, being aware of its own knowledge and able to use it in a range of arenas. For those involved in school education, this demands that the knowledge thus created be available to make a difference in society. The community of practice model described here applies equally in situations of face-to-face communication and telecommunication. The traditional isolation of the teacher must change to a more collegial approach to learning and communicating. The resources of the whole world are available through communication technology, and by using this technology, educators can benefit from and contribute to the global knowledge sharing that is now possible.

In a project with preservice teachers, McNair and Marshall (2006, p. 476) captured this intention when they defined a professional ePortfolio as "a digital profile of teaching experiences and reflections through which a community of practitioners can engage in online professional dialogue and support." They found that a first-year teacher's ePortfolio could be used as a means of making resources, such as worksheets and other teaching media, available to more experienced teachers, thereby sharing knowledge.

TOOLS FOR GLOBAL COMMUNICATION

The explosion of telecommunication has led to many opportunities for connection across the globe. E-mail transcends time zone constraints and the costs of communicating to faraway places via phone, making it a good vehicle for discussions and idea sharing. Participating in a chat or discussion group can also introduce teachers to the teaching and learning experiences of people all over the world. Various discussion groups for those interested in portfolios can be found on the Internet. Keep in mind that these discussion groups are in a global forum, where timeframes, experiences, and customs are different for everyone. To find a chat or discussion group, you can search the Internet using *ePortfolio* as a keyword. Some discussions take place in real time and are organized in advance. In this case, a calendar of topics will be available.

Blogs are becoming increasingly popular as tools are developed to make it easy to combine text, images, and links to other Web pages. *Blogging* has entered the lexicon as a term similar to diary writing. Many blogs are more interactive than paper-based diaries in that they encourage comments from readers. Other blogs have restricted access set by the creator. It is possible to find several instances of people blogging about portfolios, but few blogs are the same as portfolios. In some cases, blogging software (see www.blogger.com) might be used to create a portfolio, and parts of a blog might well be used in a portfolio as evidence or reflection.

A wiki is a democratic type of Web site that is open to all and allows anyone to edit content quickly and easily, sometimes without the need for registration. This ease of interaction and operation makes a wiki an effective tool for collaborative writing and sharing of ideas. Generally, there is no moderation of items posted. Unlike blogs, wikis are not controlled by their creators.

Some portfolio software is designed to encourage collaboration by providing a workspace for users. For example, in Australia the Victorian Technical and Further Education sector provides an ePortfolio Web site for staff and students, with private and public spaces for storing, manipulating, and sharing information. A member can invite others into a group space for collaborative activity and publish content to the Web. The portfolio developer can also choose the level of networking he or she is comfortable with.

Globally, there is growing interest in large-scale ePortfolio projects. Institutions, states, and nations are using a variety of home-grown, commercial, and open-source software, and many are keen to receive feedback or engage in discussion with those who are actually creating portfolios. Table 8.1 lists some of the Web sites that enable global communication.

WEB SITES ABOUT ePORTFOLIOS

Table 8.1   Web Sites and Organizations Involved in Portfolio Development

Host	Focus	Contact
Helen Barrett, USA	Reflection, hardware, software, blog, links	http://electronicportfolios.org
David Tosh, Elgg, UK	Software tools for social networking, blogs, links with people	http://elgg.net/
European Institute for E-Learning (EIfEL), France	ePortfolio software tool, events	www.eife-l.org
SURF, Netherlands	ePortfolios in universities	http://www.surf.nl/en/publicaties/
University of Auckland, New Zealand	Leadership development site	http://www.firstprincipals.ac.nz/portfolio.htm
TAFE, Australia	ePortfolio software tool	http://eport.tafevc.com.au/
ePortConsortium, USA	Higher education and commercial	http://www.eportconsortium.org/
Joint Information Systems Committee (JISC), UK	Technical issues, reports	www.jisc.ac.uk
Carnegie Foundation, USA	ePortfolio software tool (KEEP Toolkit)	http://www.carnegiefoundation.org/programs/sub asp?key=38&subkey=115
Centre for International ePortfolio Development, UK	Project reports	http://www.nottingham.ac.uk/eportfolio/
Learning Innovations Forum (LIFIA), Canada	Consumer guide to ePortfolios	www.lifia.ca http://www.lifia.ca/en/learn_eport_info_guides.htm
Open Source Portfolio Initiative (OSPI)	ePortfolio software tool, discussion	www.osportfolio.org groups.osportfolio.org
Education Canada	Recruitment	http://educationcanada.com/inside.phtml?a=15&eID =189
ePortfolios, UK	Project reports, sample tool	http://www.eportfolios.ac.uk
Wikipedia	Definitions, links	http://en.wikipedia.org/wiki/EPortfolio

Interacting with the online learning community provides teachers with a global perspective as people from many countries communicate without ever meeting each other in person. Electronic networking can also provide opportunities for teachers to work together globally on projects, to get feedback on professional development activities, or even to plan international exchange visits. Putting a finished portfolio on the Web can also open up dialogue with the global community. Chapter 9 discusses how educators and administrators can integrate this type of learning into their schools.

Enhancing Change Through Digital Portfolio Development

What do we wish for? That every citizen, at birth, will be granted a cradle-to-grave, lifetime personal Web space that will enable connections among personal, educational, social and business systems.

                                ~ Cohn and Hibbitts (2004)

What is the power of portfolio development? For individuals, it includes knowing what they know and how they learn. It reveals and develops a range of literacies in both teachers and students. It prepares them for their new roles in the 21st century.

NEW ROLES FOR TEACHERS

Hargreaves (1994) envisages schools in the future to be staffed by a core of "portfolio teachers": full-time, highly trained teachers supported by a range of assistants and part-time teachers who also cross employment boundaries to work in other fields. This model of teaching, reflecting Handy's (1989) portfolio worker, allows a range of contract options, including the employment of experienced teachers who do not want full-time retirement. In addition, Beare (2001) suggests that all students will have one or more online mentors whom they can access for consultation or advice about their learning programs. In this scenario, the collective competencies of teachers will benefit learners, and the collective ability of a school to make a difference will depend on its ability to pool knowledge and manage what is distributed within the organization and eventually beyond, in a network model.

Most discussion around ePortfolios assumes an individualized approach to their production, with very little focus on creating collective ePortfolios in a collaborative manner. However, this would be a legitimate social constructivist activity that schools could engage in, depending on the purpose of the task (Hartnell-Young, 2006).

Portfolios have the potential to present the collective store of knowledge of a group or organization to a wider audience and to support corporate memory in times of change. Because the knowledge economy depends on access to and sharing of knowledge, ePortfolios can serve as containers of knowledge products that reflect the learning processes needed to construct them. Their purpose then becomes broader than showcasing achievements or employability: For the individual creator they can capture a learning journey, and for society they can contribute to knowledge building by communicating knowledge from the mind into the world.

The learning organization is made up of many individual learners moving forward to achieve personal and organizational goals. The portfolio approach has the capacity to support organizational objectives through its structure, whether the purpose is for professional development planning, performance review, or employment application. The elements that form the framework for the portfolio can be based on or include reference to an organization's strategic goals. Where evaluation rubrics require reference to strategic goals, individuals must reflect on their contributions to these goals. When information is recorded in a portfolio, organizations can ascertain whether individuals are aligning with strategic goals and thus can achieve a clearer sense of staff capabilities and achievements.

For a school, the ability to provide evidence that it is doing its job—educating students—is important. This evidence can be sourced from the rich portfolios of the individual teachers (and students) and from external statistical sources. Barrett makes the point clearly in a blog entry:

> It is not really enough in today's climate just to jump through the hoops. Schools must build a culture of evidence. No longer is society content to accept the school's word that students are well educated and prepared for college or career. Schools must provide evidence that they are doing what they say they are doing—that their mission is, in fact, being fulfilled—that students really do have the skills and knowledge base they claim they have. (Barrett, 2005)

In order to meet the sometimes competing demands of individuals and organizations, Barrett and Wilkerson (2004) have suggested a conceptual framework consisting of three systems: a digital archive, a learner-centered portfolio using the learner's authentic voice, and an institution-centered database to collect relevant aggregated data. If a school or school authority were to address all three, the choice of software would necessitate a clear understanding of the goals of each system. Trials of currently available software should be undertaken before any decisions are made.

For an education system, portfolios can provide evidence, in a richer form than standardized tests, that the money invested in education is achieving results. Many educators believe that portfolios have the capacity to support professional growth and change. However, it is ironic that for a concept so linked to the notion of evidence, the evidence for the claims of portfolios themselves is limited.

In the words of Zeichner and Wray

Despite the current popularity of teaching portfolios, there have been very few systematic studies of the nature and consequences of their use for either assessment or development purposes. (2001, p. 615)

Similarly, Carney asks

Are portfolios effective devices for representing, developing, and assessing knowledge, as proponents claim? And if so, under what conditions? (2004, p. 2)

There is clearly a need for more research into the whole process of developing portfolios, from purpose to outcomes. An action research model (Kemmis, 1999) that involves practitioners is a suitable reflective approach. McNair and Marshall note that when some of their preservice students took up positions in schools, they continued the portfolio process. One commented

I have been developing my ePortfolio as part of my induction. . . . The actual practice of putting together the ePortfolio made me push myself further than I would have. (McNair & Marshall, 2006, p. 479)

In another school, a first-year teacher reported that the experience displayed through portfolio development was valued at the school:

I explained that I had completed an ePortfolio and the interview panel seemed very interested, it was from here that the Head asked to see the work when I got the job and asked me to become involved in the whole school's e-learning program. (McNair & Marshall, 2006, p. 480)

On the other hand, many of the beginning teachers felt that schools needed to be more proactive in initiating dialogue based on their portfolios. One commented

I feel that if the schools [examined] it more they would realize that it is an untapped resource that would be useful for the whole school, teachers and pupils. (McNair & Marshall, 2006, p. 481)

Another stated

[ePortfolios] will become more relevant when the schools learn how to use them properly. (McNair & Marshall, 2006, p. 481)

IMPLEMENTING A PORTFOLIO APPROACH

When conducting research for this book, we found many administrators, school leaders, and classroom teachers who would like to be more involved in a portfolio approach to developing a learning organization. They expressed great interest in the possibility of linking professional development in technology with portfolio creation. It is important to remember that a portfolio approach to professional growth is an innovation. Green and Smyser (1996) suggest that a planning timeline of at least 3 years should be allowed for complete implementation of a portfolio approach in a school, beginning with a pilot project that includes teacher training and partnering for work on development of the portfolios. The teachers in the pilot project then become mentors to the next group.

As with any innovation, it is wise to take time to spread the process throughout the school. Begin with teachers who are ready to try something new and encourage them to share their experiences and knowledge with other teachers. During this process, the focus is on the meaning of good teaching, aspects of such teaching, and verifiable evidence of good teaching. This type of focus can be achieved through discussion, consideration of values and vision through portfolio development, and self-reflection and feedback from others. Our experience of devising a professional development program that provided face-to-face interaction supported by a Web site and an e-mail list for the continual sharing of ideas and questions showed that time and resources must be set aside for this purpose if it is to be successful.

The individual and the community benefit most from the portfolio development process when there are opportunities for collaboration during production, presentation to audiences, and feedback. For example, in one school, teachers are invited to prepare portfolios for performance review, but it is not a requirement. Once each term, a week is planned to focus on professional development, share success stories, and engage in development planning. Students are also required to prepare portfolios that focus on their growth through learning. The school principal models learning to the staff and students by keeping a learning journal and maintaining a professional portfolio. Teachers in performance assessment teams are encouraged to discuss and share their portfolios. In this school, the portfolio approach has been developed over several years as a natural behavior of a learning community. In some cases, networks between schools have been developed to encourage support for portfolio development while allowing the sharing of ideas and development of joint school projects.

LIFELONG LEARNING THROUGH TECHNOLOGY

In the first ePortfolio Australia conference, held in 2004, digital portfolio projects from students and teachers in primary, secondary, vocational, and higher education sectors were presented, offering a lifelong learning perspective often missing from single-sector discussions. In the discussions about portfolios that support lifelong learning, there is some confusion as to whether people mean that they should have one portfolio for life. It is our view that throughout life people will have many portfolios, but they will be able to gain access to their archive from a variety of devices.

The 21st century requires a vision of a learning community where all learners are engaged, where teachers are learners and learners are teachers. School communities that have already developed such a vision are well prepared for this new era.

Technology must be accessible, challenging, and useful if learners are to become active producers. Broadband has opened up fast, efficient telecommunication networks to many, but there are still vast areas without such connections.

With clear goals, focusing first on the learning and then on the technology, it is less likely that vast sums of money will be spent on technology that does not support learning. Augmenting teacher and student learning with technology can empower both teachers and students by placing the control in their hands. Designers of digital portfolio systems will benefit from the collective input of teachers and students in designing systems that enable planning, use of a wide range of artifacts, scaffolding of the processes of reflection and feedback, learning assessment, and a range of presentation styles.

Dewey (1910) said that knowledge is the construction of people, and learning is the process of creating knowledge. Much later, Bereiter and Scardamalia (1998) told us that knowledge must be in the world rather than in the mind. Accordingly, we should focus on developing ePortfolio systems that support individual and collaborative learning through the very creation of ePortfolios, leading to containers of knowledge that can be shared globally. As well as focusing on individual notions of identity, learning, and employability, we should aim for "sociable ePortfolios": those that cross boundaries, informing others, with the purpose of adding to global understanding (Hartnell-Young, 2006). This type of multilayered ePortfolio can serve many different purposes for the profession of teaching, such as recording evolving understandings of teaching over time, supporting intergenerational learning in programs for induction and mentoring, and acting as a memoir, a legacy to the profession (Ellis, 2004).

Cohn and Hibbitts (2004) imagine a lifelong Web-based system that seamlessly links with past experiences (e.g., university course Web sites) and global resources (e.g., distributed experts). They suggest that, even after death, the system could survive as a record of a person's life and work, similar to Serge Ravet's dream of a "Bluetooth-enabled tombstone" (ePortfolio Australia, 2004). We believe that the value of digital portfolios is as much in their contribution to learning here and now as in recording professional and personal histories for the future.

Glossary

animation   The technique of making an image come alive through the use of movements or actions.

artifact   A specific piece of evidence contained in the personal archive. These pieces are linked together to develop a professional portfolio.

blog (Web log)   Online diary format allowing users to input text and images.

Bluetooth   A means of connecting devices (e.g., computer to computer) wirelessly over a distance of up to 10 meters.

bookmark   This is also called "Favorites" and allows the user to save the URLs of favorite sites for easy return in the future.

broadband   A telecommunication line capable of sending and receiving large amounts of data at high speed.

browser   Software that allows computers to read HTML documents and graphics and also allows Internet access. Some common browsers are Microsoft Internet Explorer and Netscape Navigator.

CD-R   Compact disk–recordable disks are similar to music CDs. They can be used in one session to store large amounts of digitized data for repeated access.

CD-RW   Compact disk–rewritable disks can be used over several sessions to store digitized data.

cellphone	A small telephone device wirelessly connected to a digital or analogue network.
chat (online)	Conversation that is carried out through messages written back and forth in real time over the Internet.
concept map	A graphic organizer designed to show links between concepts.
database	An electronic storage system used for large amounts of information that is organized into categories to make retrieval easier.
digitized (digital) data	Information that has been saved in digitized form from audio and video recordings, graphics, and still and moving images.
DVD	A high-density compact disk for storing large amounts of data, especially high-resolution audiovisual material, including moving images.
e-mail	Electronic mail, an Internet service through which the user can send and receive messages.
FTP	File Transfer Protocol, a method of transferring files to and from an Internet server.
GIF	Graphic Interchange Format, used for compressed files that are in indexed color mode (8-bit color). All graphic Web browsers support this format.
home page	The first page in a Web site; the introduction.
http	Hyper Text Transfer Protocol, a method of transferring hypertext documents.
hypertext	Links in a document that lead to other documents. Hypertext allows the user to link various pieces of text or information to various other pieces of text or information.
Internet	The shared global computing network. It provides the platform for Web services and the World Wide Web. The Internet is accessible through computers via modems.
iPod	A portable device for recording, organizing, transmitting, manipulating, and reviewing text, data, audio, image, and video files.
ISP	Internet service provider, a company or agency that sells accounts (such as dial-up or

broadband) that allow people to connect to the Internet.

JPEG	A file compression format for the Web that optimizes color images and tones.
laptop	A small but powerful computer that weighs no more than a textbook. It can be powered by a battery or an AC/DC power supply.
listserv	An electronic mailing list on which subscribers can send messages to and receive messages from all other subscribers.
memory stick (flash drive, thumb drive)	A very small storage device for digital files that connects to a computer through a USB port.
metadata, metatagging	A way of labeling digital files that enhances the capacity to search for them.
modem	A device used to connect computers to telecommunication networks. The modem electronically converts computer-generated information, which is then relayed across telephone lines.
multimedia	A general term that covers the combination of text, graphics, sound, and video in digital form.
PDF	Portable Document Format, which allows documents such as magazines to be read in original formats. Such files are often read using Adobe Acrobat Reader.
Pocket PC	A handheld device manufactured by Palm® and used to store digital material.
rubric	A set of categories used as a guide to assessment.
scanner	A device used to copy pages of text, still photographs, or diagrams into a computer. The scanned documents can then be included in a digital presentation or printed publication.
search engine	A sophisticated World Wide Web tool that compiles indexes of information found on the Internet using keywords or phrases. The search engine provides the user with a list of matches for the keyword.

server

A computer, often centralized in an institution, using software that allows information to be stored and sent to dispersed Internet users.

storyboard

A graphic organizer that indicates the relationship between files in a Web site or digital portfolio.

synchronous and asynchronous communication

In synchronous communication, interaction occurs in real time (e.g., a telephone conversation). In asynchronous communication, there is a time difference between the message and the reply (e.g., facsimiles or e-mail).

URL

Uniform Resource Locator, the World Wide Web address for a document. The URL is made up of the protocol, host name, path, and filename (e.g., http://rmit, edu.au, index.html).

video-conferencing

A telecommunication link that includes video in addition to telephony. Participants at each site need a video camera and a monitor (screen).

Web log (see *blog*)

World Wide Web

A system of Internet servers that supports HTML documents. It supports links to other documents, as well as graphics, audio, and video files.

Bibliography

Association for Supervision and Curriculum Development (ASCD). (1996, December). Teacher portfolios: Tools for improving teaching and learning. *Education Update, 38,* 1–6.

Baird, J. (1991). Individual and group reflection as a basis for teacher development. In P. Hughes (Ed.), *Teachers' professional development* (pp. 95–113). Hawthorn, Australia: ACER.

Ball, D. L., & Cohen, D. (1999). Developing practice, developing practitioners. In L. Darling-Hammond & G. Sykes (Eds.), *Teaching as the learning profession* (pp. 3–32). San Francisco, CA: Jossey-Bass.

Baron, C. (1996). *Creating your digital portfolio: A guide to marketing and self-promotion.* Indianapolis, IN: Hayden.

Barrett, H. (2004). *Electronic portfolios as digital stories of deep learning.* Retrieved April 23, 2006, from http://electronicportfolios.org/digistory/epstory.html

Barrett, H. (2005). *A high school inquiry.* Retrieved July 20, 2006, from http://electronicportfolios.org/blog/2005/02/high-school-inquiry.html

Barrett, H., & Carney, J. (2005). *Conflicting paradigms and competing purposes in electronic portfolio development.* Retrieved April 23, 2006, from http://electronicportfolios.org/portfolios/LEAJournal-BarrettCarney.pdf

Barrett, H., & Wilkerson, J. (2004). *Conflicting paradigms in electronic portfolio approaches.* Retrieved July 18, 2006, from http://www.electronicportfolios.com/systems/paradigms.html

Bartlett, A., & Sherry, A. (2004). Non–technology-savvy preservice teachers' perceptions of electronic teaching portfolios. *Contemporary Issues in Technology and Teacher Education, 4*(2), 225–247.

Baume, D. (2001). *A briefing on assessment of portfolios.* York, UK: Learning and Teaching Support Network Generic Centre.

Baume, D., Yorke, M., & Coffey, M. (2004). What is happening when we assess, and how can we use our understanding of this to improve assessment? *Assessment and Evaluation in Higher Education, 29*(4), 451–477.

Beare, H. (2001). *Creating the future school.* London: Routledge Falmer.

Bereiter, C., & Scardamalia, M. (1998). Rethinking learning. In D. Olson & N. Torrance (Eds.), *The handbook of education and human development: New models of learning, teaching and schooling* (pp. 485–514). Cambridge, MA: Blackwell.

Bridges, W. (1997). *Jobshift.* New York: Addison-Wesley.

Brown, G., & Irby, B. (1995, April). The portfolio: Should it also be used by administrators? *NASSP Bulletin,* 82–85.

Brown, G., & Irby, B. (1997). *The principal portfolio.* Thousand Oaks, CA: Corwin Press.

Burke, K. (1996a). *Designing professional portfolios for change.* Melbourne: Hawker Brownlow Education.

Burke, K. (Ed.). (1996b). *Professional portfolios: A collection of articles.* Melbourne: Hawker Brownlow Education.

Burke, K., Fogarty, R., & Belgrad, S. (1994). *The mindful school: The portfolio connection.* Melbourne: Hawker Brownlow Education.

Calderhead, J., & Gates, P. (Eds.). (1993). *Conceptualizing reflection in teacher development.* London: Falmer.

Cambridge, B., Kahn, S., Thompkins, D., & Yancey, K. (Eds.). (2001). *Electronic portfolios: Emerging practices in student, faculty, and institutional learning.* Washington, DC: American Association of Higher Education.

Cambridge, D. (2003). Video presentation from ePortfolio 2003, Poitiers, France. Retrieved April 23, 2006, from http://www .canalc2.tv/recherche.asp?idfiche=2248&btRechercher=btRecher cher&mots= ePortfolio

Campbell, D., Cignetti, P., Melenyzer, B., Nettles, D., & Wyman, R. (1997). *How to develop a professional portfolio: A manual for teachers.* New York: Allyn & Bacon.

Carney, J. (2004). *Setting an agenda for electronic portfolio research: A framework for evaluating portfolio literature.* Paper presented at the American Educational Research Association Annual Meeting, San Diego. Retrieved July 18, 2006, from http://it.wce.wwu.edu/ carney/Presentations/AERA04/AERAresearchlit.pdf

Case, S. H. (1994, October). Will mandating portfolios undermine their value? *Educational Leadership,* 46–47.

Cerbin, W. (1995, January–February). Connecting assessment of learning to improvement of teaching through the course portfolio. *Assessment Update, 7,* 4–6.

Chang Barker, K. (2003). *ePortfolio quality standards: An international development project.* Retrieved April 23, 2006, from http:// electronicportfolios.org/digistory/epstory.html

Cohn, E., & Hibbitts, B. (2004). *Beyond the electronic portfolio: A lifetime personal Web space.* Retrieved April 23, 2006, from www.edu cause.edu/apps/eq/eqmo4/eqm0441.asp

Cope, B., & Kalantzis, M. (Eds.). (2000). *Multiliteracies: Literacy learning and the design of social futures.* London: Routledge.

Covey, S. (1992). *Principal-centered leadership.* New York: Simon & Schuster.

Culham, R. E. (1996). *Alternative assessment: Portfolios from the inside out.* Portland, OR: Northwest Regional Educational Laboratory.

Day, C. (1999). *Developing teachers: The challenges of lifelong learning.* London: Falmer.

Dewey, J. (1910). *How we think.* Boston: Heath.

Diez, M. (1996). The portfolio: Sonnet, mirror and map. In K. Burke (Ed.), *Professional portfolios: A collection of articles.* Melbourne: Hawker Brownlow Education.

Dietz, M. (1998). *Journals as frameworks for change.* Thousand Oaks, CA: Corwin Press.

Educause. (2004). *Electronic portfolios: Why now?* Retrieved April 23, 2006, from www.educause.edu/ir/library/powerpoint/LIVE042 .pps

Ellis, J. (2004). *ePortfolios for professional learning.* Paper presented at the ePortfolio Australia Conference, Melbourne, Australia.

eport.consortium.org. (2003). *Electronic portfolio white paper.* Retrieved April 23, 2006, from www.eportconsortium.org/

ePortfolio Australia. (2004). *Proceedings of ePortfolio Australia Conference.* Melbourne: Author.

Europortfolio. (2006). *Europortfolio's mission.* Retrieved April 23, 2006, from http://www.eife-l.org/about/europortfolio

Fullan, M. (1995). *Change forces.* Bristol, PA: Falmer.

Gardner, H. (1984). *Frames of mind: The theory of multiple intelligences.* London: Heinemann.

Giddens, A. (1991). *Modernity and self-identity: Self and society in the late modern age.* Stanford, CA: Stanford University Press.

Green, J., & Smyser, S. (1996). *The teacher portfolio: A strategy for professional development and evaluation.* Lancaster, PA: Technomic.

Greenberg, G. (2004, July–August). The digital convergence: Extending the portfolio model. *EDUCAUSE Review,* 28–36.

Handy, C. (1989). *The age of unreason.* Boston: Harvard Business School Press.

Handy, C. (1994). *The empty raincoat: Making sense of the future.* London: Arrow Business.

Hargreaves, A., & Fullan, M. (Eds.). (1996). *Understanding teacher development.* New York: Cassell.

Hargreaves, D. (1994). *The mosaic of learning: Schools and teachers for the next century.* London: Demos.

Hargreaves, D. (2004). *Learning for life: The foundations for lifelong learning.* Bristol, UK: Policy Press.

Harrison, R. (1984). Leadership and strategy for new age. In J. Adams (Ed.), *Transforming work: A collection of organizational transformation readings.* Alexandria, VA: Miles River.

Hartnell-Young, E. (2001). Developing multimedia career portfolios in Australia: Opportunities and obstacles. *Career Planning and Adult Development Journal, 17*(3), 45–55.

Hartnell-Young, E. (2003a). *Introducing the ePortfolio: What is it? What is it for?* Video presentation from ePortfolio 2003, Poitiers, France.

Retrieved April 23, 2006, from http://www.canalc2.tv/recherche .asp?idfiche=2248&btRechercher=btRechercher&mots =ePortfolio

Hartnell-Young, E. (2003b). *Towards knowledge building: Reflecting on teachers' roles and professional learning in communities of practice.* Melbourne: The University of Melbourne. Available at http:// eprints.unimelb.edu.au/archive/00000921/

Hartnell-Young, E. (2006). ePortfolios for knowledge and learning. In A. Jafari & C. Kaufman (Eds.), *Handbook of research on ePortfolios* (pp. 125–134). Hershey, PA: Idea Publishing.

Hartnell-Young, E., & Morriss, M. (1999). Using portfolios as a vehicle for teacher professional development in technology: women@thecuttingedge. In P. Linnakylä, M. Kankaanranta, & J. Bopry (Eds.), *Portfolioita verkossa* [Portfolios on the Web] (pp. 194–208). Jyväskylä, Finland: Institute for Educational Research at the University of Jyväskylä.

Haywood, J., & Tosh, D. (2004). The e-portfolio: Supporting a European route to adult basic skills certification. *Proceedings of ePortfolio 2004 Conference* (p. 245). La Rochelle, France: European Institute for eLearning.

Home, A., & Charlesworth, A. (2004). The ePortfolio's potential as enhancer of social inclusion: Reflections on U.K. initiatives in the light of the EU e-inclusion policy. In *Proceedings of ePortfolio 2004 Conference* (p. 203). La Rochelle, France: European Institute for eLearning.

Honey, P., & Mumford, A. (1986). *The manual of learning styles.* Maidenhead, Berkshire, England: Peter Honey.

Jafari, A. (2004). The "sticky" ePortfolio system: Tackling challenges and identifying attributes. *Educause Review, 39*(4), 38.

Kane, Y. (2004). *Digital portfolios: Showcasing students as learners.* Paper presented at the ePortfolio Australia Conference, Melbourne, Australia.

Kemmis, S. (1999). Action research. In J. Keeves & G. Lakomski (Eds.), *Issues in educational research* (pp. 150–160). Oxford: Pergamon.

Kimeldorf, M. (1997). *Portfolio power: The new way to showcase all your job skills and experience.* Princeton, NJ: Peterson's Publishing Group.

Kolb, D. (1984). *Experiential learning: Experience as the source of learning and development.* Englewood Cliffs, NJ: Prentice Hall.

La Guardia Community College. *Sample portfolios.* Available at http://www.eportfolio.lagcc.cuny.edu/

Leece, R. (2005). The role of e-portfolios in graduate recruitment. *Australian Journal of Career Development, 14*(2), 72–79.

Love, D., McKean, G., & Gathercoal, P. (2004). Portfolios to webfolios and beyond: Levels of maturation. *Educause Quarterly, 27*(2), 24–37.

Lukinsky, J. (1990). Reflective withdrawal through journal writing. In J. Mezirow (Ed.), *Fostering critical reflection in adulthood* (pp. 213–234). San Francisco, CA: Jossey-Bass.

Maag, M. (2004). *The potential use of "blogs" in healthcare professionals' education.* Paper presented at the EdMedia World Conference on Educational Multimedia, Hypermedia and Telecommunications, Lugano, Switzerland.

Martin-Kniep, G. (1996). *Teachers as learners in the portfolio design process.* Sea Cliff, NY: Learner-Centered Initiatives.

McIntyre, D. (1993). Theory, theorizing and reflection in initial teacher education. In J. Calderhead & P. Gates (Eds.), *Conceptualizing reflection in teacher development* (pp. 39–52). London: Falmer.

McLaughlin, M., & Vogt, M. (1996). *Portfolios in teacher education.* Newark, DE: International Reading Association.

McLaughlin, M., & Vogt, M. (1998). *Professional portfolio models: Reflections across the teaching profession.* Norwood, MA: Christopher-Gordon.

McNair, V., & Marshall, K. (2006). How ePortfolios support development in early teacher education. In A. Jafari & C. Kaufmann (Eds.), *Handbook of research on ePortfolios* (pp. 474–485). Hershey, PA: Idea Publishing.

Mercer, N., & Fisher, E. (1998). How do teachers help children learn? An analysis of teachers' interventions in computer-based activities. In D. Faulkner, K. Littleton, & M. Woodhead (Eds.), *Learning relationships in the classroom* (pp. 111–130). London: Routledge.

Moses, B. (1997). *Career intelligence: The twelve new rules for work and life success.* San Francisco, CA: Berrett-Koehler.

New London Group. (1996). A pedagogy of multiliteracies: Designing social futures. *Harvard Educational Review, 66,* 60–92.

New Media Consortium. (2005). *A global imperative: The report of the 21st Century Literacy Summit.* Retrieved April 23, 2006, from http://www.nmc.org/pdf/Global_Imperative.pdf

Pachler, N. (2001). Connecting schools and pupils: To what end? In M. Leask (Ed.), *Issues in teaching using ICT* (pp. 15–30). London: Routledge Falmer.

Paris, S., & Ayres, L. R. (1994). *Becoming reflective students and teachers with portfolios and authentic assessment.* Washington, DC: American Psychological Association.

Paulson, F. L., & Paulson, P. (1991). *Portfolios: Stories of knowing.* Paper presented at the Annual Meeting of the Claremont Reading Conference. ERIC: ED377209.

Raymond, D., Butt, R., & Townsend, D. (1996). Contexts for teacher development. In A. Hargreaves & M. Fullan (Eds.), *Understanding teacher development.* New York: Cassell.

Rényi, J. (1996). *Teachers take charge of their learning: Transforming professional development for student success.* Washington, DC: National Foundation for the Improvement of Education.

Rifkin, J. (1994). *The end of work: The decline of the global labor force and the dawn of the post-market era.* New York: Putnam.

Roberts, G. (2006). My world: e-Portfolios: Activity and identity. *Brookes eJournal of Learning and Teaching, 1*(4). Retrieved April 23, 2006, from http://www.brookes.ac.uk/publications/bejlt/volume1 issue4/perspective/roberts.pdf

Scardamalia, M., & Bereiter, C. (1999). Schools as knowledge building organizations. In D. Keating & C. Hertzman (Eds.), *Developmental health and the wealth of nations: Social, biological and educational dynamics* (pp. 274–289). New York: Guilford.

Schön, D. A. (1983). *The reflective practitioner: How professionals think in action.* New York: Basic Books.

Schön, D. (1987). *Educating the reflective practitioner.* San Francisco, CA: Jossey-Bass.

Seldin, P. (1993). Successful use of teaching portfolios. Bolton, MA: Anker.

Seldin, P. (1997). *The teaching portfolio.* Bolton, MA: Anker.

Senge, P. (1994). *The fifth discipline: The art and practice of the learning organization.* Sydney: Random House.

Tosh, D. (2003). *ePortfolio research and development community.* Retrieved April 23, 2006, from http://www.eradc.org/

University of Auckland School Leadership Centre. (2006). *First-Time Principals Programme.* Retrieved April 23, 2006, from www.first principals.ac.nz/portfolio.htm

Wenger, E. (1998). *Communities of practice: Learning, meaning, identity.* Cambridge, UK: Cambridge University Press.

Wenger, E., McDermott, R., & Snyder, W. (2002). *Cultivating communities of practice.* Boston: Harvard Business School Press.

Wheeler, L. (1996). Getting down to business. In *The webs we weave: Experiences in on-line teaching and learning at RMIT.* Melbourne: Flexible Learning Environment Unit, RMIT University.

Wiedmer, T. (1998, April). Digital portfolios: Capturing and demonstrating skills and levels of performance. *Phi Delta Kappan,* 586–589.

Wilcox, B. (1996, November). Smart portfolios for teachers in training. *Journal of Adolescent and Adult Literacy, 40,* 172–179.

Wilkerson, J., & Lang, W. S. (2003). Portfolio, the pied piper of teacher certification assessments: Legal and psychometric issues. *Education Policy Analysis Archives, 11*(45). Retrieved July 18, 2006, from http://epaa.asu.edu/epaa/v11n45/v11n45.pdf

Winograd, P., & Jones, D. L. (1993). The use of portfolios in performance assessment. *Portfolio News, 4,* 1–13.

Wolf, K. (1994). Teaching portfolios: Capturing the complexity of teaching. In L. Ingvarson & R. Chadbourne (Eds.), *New directions in teacher appraisal.* Melbourne: ACER.

Wolf, K. (1996a). Developing an effective teaching portfolio. In K. Burke (Ed.), *Professional portfolios: A collection of articles.* Melbourne: Hawker Brownlow Education.

Wolf, K. (1996b). The schoolteacher's portfolio: Issues in design, implementation and evaluation. In K. Burke (Ed.), *Professional portfolios: A collection of articles*. Melbourne: Hawker Brownlow Education.

Wolf, K., & Siu-Runyan, Y. (1996, September). Portfolio purposes and possibilities. *Journal of Adolescent and Adult Literacy, 40*, 30–37.

Wolf, K., Whinery, B., & Hagerty, P. (1995, Spring). Teaching portfolios and portfolio conversations for teacher educators, teachers, and students. *Action in Teacher Education, 17*, 30–39.

Zeichner, K., & Wray, S. (2001). The teaching portfolio in US teacher education programs: What we know and what we need to know. *Teaching and Teacher Education, 17*, 613–621.

Index

The Corwin Press logo—a raven striding across an open book—represents the union of courage and learning. Corwin Press is committed to improving education for all learners by publishing books and other professional development resources for those serving the field of PreK–12 education. By providing practical, hands-on materials, Corwin Press continues to carry out the promise of its motto: **"Helping Educators Do Their Work Better."**